Buying

and

Selling

Antiques & Collectibles

for Fun

and Profit

Buying and Selling *Antiques & Collectibles* for Fun and Profit

By Joan & Don Bingham

Charles E. Tuttle Co., Inc.
Boston • Rutland, Vermont • Tokyo

Published in 1994 by Charles E. Tuttle Co., Inc. of Rutland, Vermont and Tokyo, Japan, with editorial offices at 153 Milk Street, Boston, Massachusetts 02109

Library of Congress Cataloging-in-Publication Data

Bingham, Joan
Buying and selling antiques and collectibles : for fun and profit / by Joan and Don Bingham.
p. cm.
Includes bibliographical references.
ISBN 0-8048-1986-6 (pbk.)
1. Antiques—Collectors and collecting. 2. Collectibles.
I. Bingham, Don, 1930– II. Title
NK1125.B5
745.1'068—dc20 94-7707
CIP

3 5 7 9 10 8 6 4 2

(M&G)
Printed in the United States of America

We'd like to thank the people at Charles E. Tuttle Company for their help with this book: Peter Ackroyd, President and C.E.O., for deciding it was right for the Tuttle list; Isabelle Bleecker, Managing Editor, for pulling it all together; and Karen Aude for a super job of editing.

Contents

Introduction

We're often asked how we happened to get into the business of buying and selling antiques and collectibles. The truth is, we started doing this as a hobby. We are, and have been all of our adult lives, writers. And writing is a solitary profession. Both of us felt the need to get out into the world more. After all, we do like people.

A good friend, who's an antiques dealer, suggested we attend a few auctions . . . just for the fun of it and because we like antiques and were, at that time, looking for furniture and accessories for our home. We took the advice and went to auctions, we saw lots of merchandise, we bought things for our house, and we thoroughly enjoyed ourselves. The only trouble was we had soon purchased everything we needed, and we still wanted to go to auctions. "Well," our friend said, "Why don't you go into the business?"

After a bit of discussion, we decided it was worth a try. We might not make money at it, but we would have fun, and we could continue to attend the auctions we had grown to love. Our initial efforts at purchasing inventory were not always successful. Before we started in business, we purchased only those things that we personally wanted to own. But once we were in business, we knew we had to get merchandise that would appeal to a variety of people.

Certain names and items were familiar to us—Limoges, Bradley and Hubbard, and Tiffany, for example.

When an item came up at auction that bore one of those familiar names, we'd bid and more often than not we'd take the item in question home—delighted with our purchase and with our knowledge. It didn't take us long to discover that Limoges (or any china) with a transfer pattern is generally worth far less than it would be if the design were handpainted. We then bid on everything we saw that was handpainted only to discover that some handpainted articles were well done and others were not, and that pieces handpainted at the factory were almost always nicer than those done by a hobbiest. We found that the name Bradley and Hubbard was a good one and did help sell an item. But we also found that articles with missing pieces were slow sellers even if they were by Bradley and Hubbard. And Tiffany—that wonderful name—it wasn't long before we discovered that most Tiffany on the market today is Tiffany type, and that anything actually done by Louis Comfort Tiffany was well out of our price range.

We continued to learn, and we found to our surprise that we were making a profit. Not a large one at first. But a profit nonetheless. We found that we did best and were happiest selling a variety of merchandise with a wide price range. We also discovered garage sales, flea markets, tag sales, and estate sales were viable markets for purchasing articles to sell, although we confess we've never enjoyed this type of shopping as much as auctions.

Our little hobby was turning into a lucrative business. We found we looked forward to our selling days. We made friends with other dealers and with customers. But most of all we were and are having fun buying and selling antiques and collectibles. We hope you do too!

To Stephen
whose courage is an inspiration

CHAPTER 1

Finding Merchandise: The Never-Ending Quest

In order to start in the antiques and collectibles business, or to stay in it, you need merchandise to sell. Obtaining that merchandise is a large part of the business. In fact, it usually proves to be the most time-consuming facet. And yet we are not alone in considering it the part of the business that's the most fun. It's a great way to satisfy your desire to shop without depleting your pocketbook, because if you make your choices wisely you're going to turn the items you purchase into a healthy profit.

Many people get started in the business when they decide they have a few things that aren't right for their homes anymore but they don't want to give them away or throw them out. They have a garage sale, count the profits, and decide this is a good way to make some extra money. Then the problem becomes—finding more merchandise.

Some people are collectors and find that they're not as enchanted with their collections as they once were. Or having collected for many years, they discover that their tastes have become more finely honed. What at one time seemed like a valuable addition to their collection is actually an inferior or common piece that would only be valued by a beginner. They pack up the unwanted pieces and send them to auction. Or they advertise them in a collector's publication. Or they decide to rent a booth or space in a market somewhere. They're pleased with the prices they get and enthusiastic about being in the business. The problem is—finding more merchandise.

A few people, some of substantial means, just love to attend auctions. They can't resist a good buy and purchase many lovely items. It doesn't take long before these people have purchased so many articles that their homes begin to overflow. Often, the answer to this overcrowding is to go into the business. These people start with the items with which they've grown tired, the things they wish they'd never purchased, or articles of which they are the least fond. They continue to attend auctions. But since they are now selling to others, as well as purchasing for themselves, the problem is—finding more merchandise.

There are, of course, other reasons why people go into the business. They may need to supplement their incomes, they may think they can live on what they make in the business by working at it full time, or they may just want the sheer fun of it. There are those who inherit an estate that includes a houseful of goods. They decide that rather than selling to a dealer or sending the merchandise to auction, they'll attempt to sell it themselves by temporarily going into the business. Once they have a taste of it, they often continue, and they face the same problem—finding more merchandise.

The Search Begins

GARAGE SALES

Spring is the best season to start your business. Most people feel that new enthusiasm that comes with the first spring buds, but, more important, it's the season when garage sales begin to happen in large numbers. People start cleaning out attics, cellars, and cabinets and begin to get rid of unwanted clutter. There may be wonderful treasures among that clutter. We've found some of our most profitable items at garage sales. There was the Hull tea set Joan purchased for one dollar and sold the very next day for ninety-five dollars to another dealer who obviously planned to mark it up even more. And one dismal Saturday morning we found five old fire company fire extinguishers, made of copper and all polished up, for four dollars a piece. We bought all five. True, they didn't sell as fast as the Hull tea set, but we did sell them—and for thirty-five dollars a piece. It was worth the wait. Don came upon a 16 mm movie camera with a fine leather case, remarkably priced at fifty cents. He put a price of fifty-five dollars on it, and it sold within a month. We could go on and on about garage sale finds, but you get the idea.

However, we don't want to lead you to believe that all your garage sale treks will result in phenomenal buys. There's many a week we come back empty-handed or with pretty average merchandise. Many dealers who've been in the business as long as we have wouldn't be caught at a garage sale. But we've found them among the best places to get items at a price that we can mark up enough to make a sizable profit.

Garage saling is an art form. Most sales take place on Friday, Saturday, or Sunday, with the lion's share being Saturday-only sales. There are sales on other days, of course, but they're not the norm. The first step is to purchase a paper and turn to the classified section. There, under the heading "Garage Sales," you'll find a varying number of listings, depending on the season and the area of the country in which you live. Friday's sales are usually in Thursday's paper. Saturday and Sunday sales generally appear in Friday's and Saturday's paper. Carefully select the sales you want to attend. To do this, first read through all the listings and cross out any in which you're not interested, such as those that read something like, "lots of modern furniture," or "clothing to fit all sizes," or "an assortment of household goods." Also, be aware that one that lists antiques may only have a couple of old, cracked, or crazed plates with high price tags on them (which you wouldn't want anyway at any price because of the damage), and a lot of junk. Generally the people who list antiques want high prices if they have anything good, and bargains are hard to find. On the other hand, people who don't know anything about antiques or collectibles often put wonderful items out at ridiculously low prices. Other listings won't be specific as to merchandise offered, and you'll have to make a choice on intuition alone.

The ad also lists the time a garage sale will begin. In our area, most sales begin at either 8:00 A.M. or 9:00 A.M. There are a few with starting times of 7:00 A.M., and even fewer that open up at 10:00 A.M. or 11:00 A.M. Circle the sales that sound interesting to you. You must plan to be at these sales at least an hour before they're scheduled to start unless the ad states "no early birds." Usually a sale is picked of all merchandise desirable to a dealer within fifteen minutes. Of course, there are instances where sleepers that are quite valuable are overlooked because they're not common enough to be known by the average dealer. But at garage sales this is the exception rather than the rule.

We always try to select two sales that are close to each other and that begin at the same time. For instance, if there's one listed at 802 Twelfth Street in Emmaus and another at 890 Fourteenth Street in the same town, and both of them are advertised as starting at 8:00 A.M., we'll be at one or the other by 7:00 A.M. If the first one we go to isn't ready for business, we'll quickly go on to the second. Then when that has opened and we've looked over the merchandise to see if we want anything, we return to our first stop.

We also circle two sales for 9:00 A.M. and two for 10:00 A.M., if any seem right for us. And we repeat the procedure we went through for the 8:00 A.M. sales.

Weather is a factor in garage sales. If it's raining, look for sales that advertise "rain or shine" or choose those that take place in church basements or school gyms. Sometimes a sale will be listed as "a whole houseful of goods." If the ad is legitimate, then the sale is an indoor sale. Few people try to put "a whole houseful of goods" on their lawn. And, of course, there are a few sales that live up to their name and are actually held in garages.

We have found that most neighborhood sales are a waste of time. Especially those listed as annual sales. To begin with, they're often in newer communities or developments, inhabited by young people who don't have anything but newer used items, wedding presents that they've never used, and baby and children's clothes outgrown by their offspring. If the development has never had a sale before, you might be lucky enough to find a piece of china or other article that has been handed down. But if the sale is annual, it's almost certain that the one piece of china was sold at the first sale.

Ideally you will find all merchandise at garage sales marked with a price. But if it isn't, this is forgivable. After all, these probably aren't professionals. Most people who have garage sales are savvy enough to realize that everyone is looking for a bargain—a break—and they mark their items accordingly, expecting to haggle a bit. We make it a practice never to ask for anything off of an item if it's priced at three dollars or under. But for items marked above this price, one of us will usually inquire if the owner can do better. Some won't budge an inch, but most will give you a break. No matter how inflated you think a price is or how inferior the merchandise, don't belittle it to its owner. This never results in anything but hurt feelings, and instead of the price break you expected and might have received otherwise, you're going to be met with understandable resentment. If we're interested in a piece and hope for a little lower price, we generally ask, "Is this your best price?" If the answer is yes, we'll say, "It's very nice, but it's a little more than we can pay for it." With this retort and a smile, we've often ended up with the article in question at the savings we'd hoped for.

Beware of the professional garage sale! Some people have garage sales frequently—some every week, others every month. These people are really dealers and some have fine merchandise. They scout the other garage sales, flea markets, and auctions. You learn to spot them after a while. It may be from seeing the same ad run frequently, or it may be from their signs, which are either very well done or look worn and well used. There's nothing wrong with professional garage sale dealers. You may find that over all they have a better grade of merchandise than you encounter at other garage sales. But you'll probably pay more because chances are they have a much greater storehouse of knowledge than the amateur. Can you get bargains from the professional? Yes, often you can, but you're not likely to find something like a Hull tea set for one dollar.

Garage sales are a gamble. You may waste an entire morning and come up empty-handed, having spent time and used up gas for nothing. On the other hand, you may have found treasures that you can mark up a hundredfold. To us, it's worth the risk.

FLEA MARKETS

The next rung up the shopping ladder is the flea market. (Sometimes it's the next step down.) Like garage sales, flea markets come in many guises. There are absolutely huge markets that sell everything from fresh vegetables to new t-shirts and sweat socks to paintings on velvet. Occasionally, you'll find a small stand that features collectibles and antiques. But what you're more likely to find are a few tables with secondhand junk. There's not much chance that you'll spot any treasures here, but if you've already made the effort to go to the market, do take the time to look through these tables, you could turn up a bargain.

Flea markets can be indoor or outdoor affairs. A flea market may be a one-time deal held by a church or an organization, or it may be a weekly or monthly sale. Those held by organizations are often peppered with dealers who are members of that organization, and the merchandise they have to offer falls in the range of what you'll find at the average garage sale—with one exception. Since they are setting up with many dealers and some of them may be professionals, anything that's really good will be gone before the sale starts, having been picked up by another dealer with a more practiced eye.

Flea markets start at various times of the morning, some as early as 4:00 A.M. For the early ones, at which there's a real feeling of adventure, you may find yourself stumbling around in a dark field. You need a bright flashlight—one of the little pocket jobs won't do the trick—so that you can carefully inspect what's on each table. Markets that begin this early are often over with by 10:00 A.M. The dealers may even pack up their wares and go on to a later market.

The flea market is a great place to sharpen your bargaining skills. If you're the shy type—afraid to ask for a price break—you're going to have to steel yourself. You can be quite certain that the dealer you're approaching seldom pays the full asking price for anything and won't be surprised or offended if you ask, "What's your best dealer price?" Saying "dealer price" is important. While many people who run garage sales resent dealers and think they have some magical ability to cheat them, those who sell at flea markets are, for the most part, dealers themselves, and they understand the problems of the business. They know that as a dealer you can't pay retail price and turn around and make a profit.

TAG SALES

In most areas of the country, there are what are known as "tag sales." These sales are generally comprised of the entire contents of an apartment, house, or estate. The seller (usually either someone who's inherited the property, or someone who's moving and doesn't want to, or can't take the merchandise with him or her), puts the task of selling the contents into professional hands. The company that's holding the sale sends representatives to the residence. These representatives appraise and tag all of the items to be sold. Remember, these people know what they're doing or they wouldn't be in business long. There are few bargains at tag sales. However, as with any other sale, some unusual treasure may surface at an unusually low price.

As a rule, tag sale customers line up outside the appointed place well in advance of the time the sale is scheduled to begin. Each person is assigned a number, and when sale time arrives, only a few people are allowed in at a time. As someone leaves, someone else enters. At the very end of a tag sale, merchandise is often available for much less than it is tagged, since the object of these sales is to sell everything at once. So you may want to visit one late in the day. Or if you're there when the sale starts and you see something that appeals to you, ask if you can leave an offer in the event the item in question doesn't sell. We usually write the item in which we're interested and the price we're offering on the back of our business card.

SECONDHAND STORES

While it could seem that secondhand stores should have little to offer antiques and collectibles dealers, this isn't always the case. And the beauty of shopping in these emporiums of used merchandise is that while secondhand dealers may know the going price for a used dining room suite, a set of Melmac plates, or a tired-looking sofa, they are seldom conversant in your field—antiques and collectibles. As a result, combing these stores can turn up wonders at give-away prices. Joan once found an old Oriental mud figure with a price tag of two dollars. This wasn't one of the many reproductions but a grand old piece. She could hardly believe her luck and quickly paid for it, feeling almost as if she were stealing. Even a reproduction mud figure is worth far more than two dollars.

Shopping the secondhand stores usually means being willing to get your hands dirty. Much of the merchandise won't be washed, and often it is stacked on shelves or on the floor so that you have to dig for it. Secondhand dealers will usually bargain, but their prices tend to be firmer than those of flea market dealers.

ARTICLES FOR SALE

Most newspapers have an "articles for sale" column in the classified section. We look at it every morning, and if there's something we think might interest us, we call immediately. Good merchandise, priced right, sells fast. Don't assume that the price listed in the paper isn't negotiable. Most people expect to bargain. If an item is really overpriced, we wait a week or more before we call. By then the ad is probably out of the paper, and the owner of the merchandise may be quite discouraged. If we see the item and we want it, we make an offer based on what it's worth to us. Sometimes it's refused, but often it's accepted.

The trade papers are another source of inventory. They publish long lists of collectibles and antiques for sale by individuals. Buying this way can be either a success or a miserable disappointment. Assuming that the owner of an item lives some distance away from you, you're going to be purchasing that item sight unseen. You should ask to see a picture. Of course, the picture may not reveal flaws that would be apparent if you were able to carefully inspect the piece, but it will help. After you've received the picture, if you still want to go ahead with the purchase, you should get a guarantee of condition in writing signed by the seller. You will probably receive the article C.O.D., so you won't have a chance to inspect it before you pay for it.

Some things are less chancy to purchase in this manner. For instance, any of the limited edition plates, figurines, etc. are fairly safe. Providing they're in the condition the seller says they are, you'll be in for no surprises. After all, a 1982 Bing and Grondahl plate is a 1982 Bing and Grondahl plate. You've seen one, you've seen them all. There might be a slight color variation, but not enough to make much difference. However, if the merchandise you're interested in is, say, a pair of art deco bookends, you may find they're smaller than they looked in a picture, or that they don't have as much detail as you'd expected, or that they're lighter in weight than you'd hoped.

Before you offer anything for sale, be sure it's clean and in as good condition as you can make it. Chapter 5 deals with cleaning and repairing and will help you to keep your merchandise in tip-top shape.

PICKERS

Pickers are people (usually very knowledgeable in at least some types of antiques and collectibles) who make their living by obtaining merchandise they know they can immediately turn over to dealers. They frequent auctions, flea markets, tag sales, and secondhand shops just as the dealers do, but they know what they're looking for and to whom they can sell it. If you specialize in a certain type of merchandise or you're looking for, say, a pair of old Royal Dux lamps, you may want to ask a picker to look for you. You won't profit as much as you would if you found the lamps yourself, but you also won't spend all that time looking. Pickers have connections—the better the connections, the more likely they are to find what any given dealer wants. Any pickers I've known have been meticulous in examining merchandise before they buy. They go over every inch of a piece several times looking for flaws or repairs. Not much will miss the eye of an experienced picker.

OTHER DEALERS

One good turn deserves another, and if you sell at a co-op or are acquainted with many other dealers (which you will almost certainly be as you progress in the business), you may strike a deal with one or several of them. Suppose there's a dealer in your co-op who specializes in Avon collectibles, one who carries McCoy cookie jars, and another who likes to have a large assortment of salt and peppers in her booth. You, on the other hand, really don't care for these things but are wildly enthusiastic about Atkinson Fox prints. When you go to garage sales, flea markets, or auctions you can look for Avon, McCoy cookie jars, and salt and pepper shakers to sell to the other dealers at exactly what you pay for them, and they, in turn, can look for Fox prints to sell to you at cost. Of course, you need to get together to discuss this, exchanging information on what to look for (Avon should be in its original box with product, if possible; McCoy should be marked on the bottom; advertising salt and peppers, nodders, miniatures, turn arounds, and nesters are a few types of salt and peppers that are worth more than just ordinary figurals; Fox prints should be signed, in good condition, and in the original frame). And, of course, everyone needs to know just how much the other dealer is willing to pay for merchandise.

You will find that the kinds of things that sell in one region don't move very well in another area. If you know what's hot in your market, you should be able to purchase merchandise from other dealers in areas where those items may be almost impossible to move. Most dealers will give at least a ten percent discount to other dealers. And since no one in this business knows everything there is to know, you may visit a shop or co-op and find a piece that has much more value than that placed on it by the owner of the merchandise.

DIRECT CONTACTS

One of the best ways to obtain merchandise, and one of the more advanced approaches, is to buy the entire contents of a house. Of course, the house has to have some desirable things in it for it to be worth your while, and this isn't something you're likely to have either the funding or the know-how to do when you're just beginning. It is, however, a lucrative venture when it's approached correctly.

Some people who inherit estates are willing to turn the entire job of getting rid of the contents over to someone else. They don't want to clean. They don't want to sort through things. They don't want to arrange for the appraisal of items. They just want the money and no hassles, thank you. These people will sell you the entire contents with the understanding that you'll get it all out of the house, which they are probably going to sell. Sometimes they want the house cleaned as well.

First, you must tour the house, examining the contents of every cupboard, closet, and corner. You must go up in the attic and down in the cellar. And you must, absolutely must, write down what's there. Look on the bottom of each dish and duplicate any marks on your notepad. Inquire of whomever is selling the house about anything you don't recognize or to which you cannot assign a value. Insist that the person who is selling the contents give you the price he or she wants for it. Don't make the first offer. This is good practice for two reasons. First, you may insult someone by offering a price that is far less than he or she thinks the merchandise is worth. This can result in a complete breakdown in negotiations, ending a deal that might otherwise have worked out. Second, you may make an offer that's vastly higher than the seller had anticipated and end up paying more than is necessary.

Whatever the seller has decided the merchandise is worth, tell him or her you'll report back. And before you accept or reject it (unless it's so high you know you're absolutely not going to be able to come to an agreement), find out the value of any items with which you're not familiar. If you go back to the seller with a counter offer, make it for the entire group of items that interests you. Offers on individual pieces almost always result in haggling. If your offer is for the entire contents of the house, you must determine with certainty the amount for which you can sell the items. Is it going to be worth the time and effort you'll expend? Is the merchandise clean and ready for sale or will you have to clean it all? There are bound to be some articles that are throwaways.

If things work out and you and the person who's selling the contents of the house reach an agreement, you'll be the proud owner of a houseful of articles of varying descriptions and values. It can seem overwhelming. Sort things out by category. First, select all the treasures you want for your business. You're still going to be left with a variety of items. You're not going to get anything for opened boxes of laundry detergent and the like, but you've probably signed an agreement to take care of them. Throw them out. Old clothes, unless they're vintage, can go to the rescue mission or some other local charity, as can brooms, mops, pails, etc. Any furniture that you're not going to be handling in your market can be sent to an auction. Find the right auctioneer for each item. Good antique furniture goes to a good auction where the auctioneer can get top dollar. But if the furniture is inferior or modern, it will fare better at the type of auction frequented by secondhand dealers and retail consumers than at the finer auctions where people are looking for period pieces.

A Word to the Wise

KNOW WHAT YOU'RE BUYING

In general, dealers who sell at flea markets aren't as knowledgeable as those who sell at co-ops or have their own antiques shops. So it pays for you as a buyer to use that to your advantage. The best suggestion we can give you is to read, read, read. (You'll find a list of recommended reading at the end of this book.) Learn to identify as many items as possible and learn which are the most valuable. This gives you the upper hand not only at flea markets, but when you're doing business with experienced dealers as well.

Can you learn all there is to know? It's very doubtful. In all our years in the business, we've never met anyone who knows everything about everything. There are just too many things to learn. How then can you benefit by reading? Start your education with something that interests you. Do Disney items (called Disneyana) intrigue you? Perhaps the sight of Mickey, Minnie, Donald Duck, and the other wonderful characters bring back fond memories. There are many books on Disney and several of them include price guides.

While we're on the subject, this is as good a place as any to warn you about price guides. While we consider them an important tool of the business (an opinion that is not shared by all dealers), they are only guides. The prices in them are generally taken from auctions and are often greatly inflated. The person who paid $1,000 for a stuffed Mickey Mouse may be the only person in the world who would pay that much for that particular item. The rule of thumb is that you're probably not going to get more than seventy or eighty percent of a list price, so you must buy accordingly.

But where guides can be of particular use is in preventing you from paying too much. If you see that a particular piece of Roseville pottery lists for $85, you know better than to purchase it from the dealer who's trying to convince you that it's a buy at $200. There are exceptions to this. A few specialty books do list low for what the items sell for in a particular region. For instance, salt and pepper shaker collectors who are members of a club tend to be willing to pay more than book value in my area.

Perhaps you're not interested in collectibles but wish to carry only antiques. Start reading about what catches your fancy the most. Maybe it's Nippon china. Find a book. There are many of them. Photocopy the pages with the identifying back marks (a good book will tell you the years during which these marks were used), and when you go to buy merchandise, check the marks on the particular piece in which you're interested against the marks on the photocopied sheet.

BEWARE OF FAKES

You may even find that the piece you're considering is a fraud—a recent, inferior piece made to mimic an older, more valuable one. Entire warehouse-type, dealer-only establishments are packed with an amazing assortment of new merchandise designed to fool the retail customer. A trip to one of these places is a fine idea as it will open your eyes and help you avoid being a victim. We visit the warehouse in our vicinity about twice a year—not to buy, but to study. On one occasion we found a vase that was identical in all respects—markings and all—to one for which we'd eagerly paid three times the price at an auction. But we were lucky. After seeing that we'd been duped, we marked the vase a reproduction and repriced it at a few dollars more than we'd paid for it. It quickly sold, but it sold for what it was—a reproduction.

Perhaps this is the place to touch on the ethics of selling a reproduction as authentic. We know that some dealers think "all is fair in love and antiques." We don't share that opinion for two reasons. One, it's dishonest. And two, it's a business practice that will repay you with a perfidious reputation.

A Word to the Wise

SELECTING A SPECIALTY

Wouldn't it be nice to be the only antiques and/or collectibles dealer in your area? There's a lot to be said in favor of having a monopoly—ask the old-timers at Xerox, AT&T, and IBM. They'll tell you, you have to pull out all the stops when competition enters the arena. You can bet your boots that the operating costs for running power companies would be drastically reduced in order to lower utility rates if consumers could go elsewhere. In our business, consumers can, and do, go elsewhere, and you can only lower prices so far. So in order to entice more customers to cross your threshold and spend their money with you, you need an edge, a plus, something special. And that's what we advise, give the customers something special—your specialty!

We don't mean that you should carry only one type of merchandise. That can and does work for some dealers, but it is usually a lonely life waiting for those few, select customers. What we're advocating is that you find a speciality to sell along with your general merchandise.

If you're already a collector of something beyond family mementos, that collectible could be your speciality. If not, look around at what collectibles and special lines other dealers in your market carry and find something different. It should be something you are interested in and can talk about with enthusiasm. There should be a demand for it. (Sundials are a fascinating collectible, but how many people collect them?) Learn all you can about your specialty. Buy books on the subject, or borrow them from the public library. Get a current price guide. Then purchase examples of your speciality whenever possible, even if you have to spend a little more money at the beginning. That is, be willing to make less profit at first in order to start the ball rolling.

BE ALERT TO CHANGE

Change is certain. Be aware that the antiques and collectibles market is always evolving. For a year or two, Victorian wares are in, then maybe it's post-WW II modern, followed next by Arts and Crafts, and so on. Interest in the various collectibles also waxes and wanes. As of this writing, Avon and Jim Beam bottles are no longer the rage they were a few years ago, while dolls and toy trucks continue to climb in popularity. An increase in the number of buyers for a given item creates higher prices, which in turn decreases the available supply. If the number of buyers declines, or the supply is inflated above the demand, prices will fall.

In 1985 we met a couple whose speciality was depression and carnival glass. In fact, they had very little else in their booth. Their selection was extraordinary and sales were brisk. However, by early 1988 sales had decreased so badly that the couple was not making the rent. They pulled out of the mall in the fall of 1988 and sent their merchandise to auction.

A Word to the Wise

Two related factors had developed between 1985 and the demise of the couple's business. First, reproductions of depression and carnival glass were flooding the market. Collectors and dealers alike couldn't always tell if the items were originals or reproductions. Second, because of the reproductions (and possibly also because depression and carnival glass had peaked as collectibles in the couple's area), interest in those items declined. The result was that while prices for original pieces remained stable, overall demand dwindled.

Had this couple been set up in another market or area, perhaps their sales would have continued at a high volume. But they weren't, and they illustrate what can happen when you put all your eggs in one basket.

Early on in the business, Joan was drawn to Limoges. She bought a book about it and spent hours studying it. She looked for Limoges at garage sales, auctions, flea markets, and other antiques outlets. At first she bought anything marked Limoges. Then with familiarity came selectivity. She bypassed the transfer designs and zeroed in on hand-painted pieces. Then she discovered that all hand-painted pieces weren't created equal. She also learned that all Limoges isn't marked *Limoges.* Many of the early pieces just have a factory mark. She also found that all Limoges wasn't made in France. It wasn't too long before our booth became the first place people headed when they wanted a good piece of Limoges. We don't carry much Limoges anymore. It's become extremely difficult to find quality Limoges at affordable prices. We've become interested in handling well-executed oil paintings. They don't have to be by listed artists (although that's certainly a plus), but they must have eye-appeal.

We advise you to find that special something for which you feel an affinity. Learn about it, buy it, sell it, but don't overstock and don't make it your only, or even your primary, type of merchandise.

CHAPTER 2

Identifying Antiques: A Primer for Beginners and Intermediates

When you're shopping for antique merchandise, it's important to know what to look for in any given item. Some pieces scream quality. Somehow, without knowing just what they are, you know they're valuable. But by and large you need to have an idea of exactly what it is you're seeking. We find that some of the most highly prized antiques appear plain and uninteresting.

The purpose of this book is to help you get into the business and make a go of it, not to acquaint you with all of the merchandise you're likely to encounter over the years. The longer you're in the business, the more familiar you'll become with the many types of items you'll find. And as we've said previously, unless you're a very unusual person, you'll never know everything. But that's the beauty of it—it's an ongoing learning experience.

In the beginning, you should stick to antiques that are easily identifiable—pieces that you can feel certain are what they appear to be. Toward that end, you may want to study the following list. It's comprised of items that you are likely to find in your search for merchandise and includes information to help you learn to recognize them. The dates we supply are as accurate as we were able to make them. Experts in the various specialties often differ about exactly when merchandise was produced.

Glass, Porcelain, and Pottery

ABC PLATES

Made of glass, metal, porcelain, or pottery, ABC Plates were in vogue in the 1700s and 1800s. Each plate displays the letters of the alphabet. They were used to help teach children their ABC's. Often you'll find modern versions at garage sales, but unless they're several decades old, they're of little value on the market. Even those dating back to the 1930s or 1940s are worth far less than the old ones.

AMERICAN ENCAUSTIC TILES

These decorative tiles were made by the American Encaustic Tiling Company from 1875 until 1935 when the factory closed. (It was reopened as Shawnee Pottery Company in 1937 and closed permanently in 1960.) Each tile is marked with a stylized *A T* and an *O* within a *C.*

AURENE GLASS

An iridescent blue or gold glass made into bottles, bowls, candlesticks, vases, etc., in the early 1900s by

Frederick Carder, most pieces of Aurene glass are marked either *Aurene* or *Steuben,* often with a paper label. This glass is quite valuable, but on occasion a piece will surface at a garage sale held by someone who is ignorant of its worth.

BAVARIAN PORCELAIN

The word *Bavaria* appears in the backstamp of most Bavarian pieces. If the mark also says *Germany,* then the piece was probably made after 1871. Bavarian porcelain was sometimes decorated by hand, and sometimes by use of the transfer method. A good hand-painted decoration is the most valuable.

BEEHIVE MARK

Many people get excited when they see a mark that resembles a beehive on the back of a piece of porcelain. Sometimes that excitement is warranted, sometimes it isn't. The original beehive mark was used by the Royal Porcelain Manufactory of Vienna, beginning in the early 1700s. It was underglaze; most pieces were hand-decorated and are highly valued. However, the beehive mark has been copied on cheap, transfer-decorated items. And on most of these pieces, the beehive is *over* the glaze. Incidentally, even though the mark is called beehive by dealers, it actually was designed to depict a shield.

BENNINGTON WARE

During the 1800s, two factories in Bennington, Vermont, produced bottles, bowls, creamers, crocks, cuspidors, inkwells, jugs, pitchers, vases and many other pottery items. A mottled finish was common. Most pieces were marked *Bennington* and so are easily identifiable. They are highly valued.

BRIDES' BASKETS

Glass bowls that fitted into silver-plated holders with handles were popular wedding gifts from the late 1800s until around 1905. Most of these are one-of-a-kind designs produced by American and European glass makers. You may find them in cased glass, cut glass, hand-painted glass, ruffled-edged glass, etc. Many more silver-plated holders than glass baskets have survived. The holders alone are worth far less than the complete unit, but the glass bowl alone is still quite valuable.

CAMBRIDGE POTTERY

A brown-glazed pottery made in Cambridge, Ohio, from 1898 until 1909, Cambridge Pottery bears many marks, including the outline of an acorn or the words *Oakwood,* or *Terrhea.*

CASTOR SETS

American Victorian castor sets had silver-plated holders and glass bottles intended as containers for an assortment of condiments from oil and vinegar to mustard and sugar. They became popular in the 1700s and continued as a standard item on American tables until the early part of the 1900s. In the late 1800s, the bottles were often made of colored glass. Look for sets with bottles that match and stoppers that aren't broken or missing. While wear to the silver plate detracts from a set, it doesn't render it worthless. Castor sets have been reproduced, especially those with colored bottles. Beware of the set that looks too perfect.

CASTOR, PICKLE

Standing about five- to seven-inches high, ornate pickle jars fit into silver holders with arching handles similar in style to those found on brides' baskets. Each holder has a hook on which a pickle fork rests. Pickle castors were the rage for about ten years from the late 1800s until the early 1900s. Look for examples with the glass jar and the pickle fork still intact.

CLOISONNE

The type of cloisonne that you're most likely to find is made by applying enamel between wires that protruded out from a metal item. Most cloisonne was, and is, made in the Orient. Much newer cloisonne is marked China and will not command the price of older cloisonne. Any damage greatly reduces the price. We've found that interest in cloisonne, and, in fact, any Orientalia, is regional. New England and the West Coast are the two areas where we have found the most interest in Orientalia.

CORALENE GLASS

This usually quite expensive glass was made by firing glass beads to glass objects. The glass beading was applied in a variety of patterns, resulting in raised designs. The process, widely used in the late 1800s, has been reproduced.

COSMOS GLASS

Produced by the Consolidated Lamp and Glass Company from 1895 until about 1915, most pieces of Cosmos glass were made in milk glass, although a few items were produced in clear glass. The most popular pattern features an array of colored flowers in raised relief designs. The process was used on everything from lamp shades to salt and pepper shakers.

CROWN MILANO

This biscuit-colored glass with satin finish was made by Frederick Shirley in the late 1800s. Adorned with flowers, Crown Milano sometimes features gold decoration. Crown Milano is usually marked with a crown over a stylized *M*. You'll find examples in tumblers, vases, biscuit jars, etc.

CUT GLASS

Many novice dealers have trouble telling the difference between cut glass and pressed. Cut glass is sharp on the edges of the pattern, while pressed glass has a smoother feel to it. Near-cut glass is pressed glass of a little better quality than most and is slightly sharper on the edges. Made in many patterns, many of the better pieces of cut glass are signed by the manufacturer. Cracks and chips are often difficult to find and are more apparent to the touch than the eye. A crack will greatly detract from the piece, but the absence of a tooth on the edge reduces the value only minimally.

DAUM NANCY

The Daum Nancy glass works was started in Nancy, France, in the late 1800s by Jean Daum. This expensive, beautifully decorated, usually cameo or etched glass, has been marked in a variety of ways, but the mark usually includes both *Daum* and *Nancy.*

DAVENPORT

The word *Davenport* on a piece of pottery or porcelain means that it was made in Staffordshire, England, at the Davenport factory, which operated from the late 1700s to the late 1800s. Davenport creamwares, earthenwares, ironstone, and porcelains were of high quality and are very desirable.

DE VEZ GLASS

This French cameo glass was made by the Cristallerie de Pantin in the late 1800s. Most pieces are signed *De Vez,* often in scroll.

DEDHAM POTTERY

First produced from 1891 to 1895 in Chelsea, Massachusetts, then in Dedham, Massachusetts, from 1895 until 1943 when the factory closed, Dedham Pottery dishes are easily identifiable, decorated with a crackleware finish and figures of animals and flowers. Most of the designs are done in dark blue and are backstamped *Dedham Pottery* with the picture of a rabbit—one of the manufacturer's most popular subjects.

DEGUE GLASS

This French cameo or smooth glass made around the turn of the century bears the acid-etched signature, *Degue.* Vases are the most commonly found pieces.

DELFT

A tin-glazed pottery with blue and white or multi-colored decorations, Delft has been made in Holland since about 1564. Windmills and tulips are common designs. Many of the older pieces aren't marked, while pieces made after the late 1800s are usually marked *Holland.*

DOULTON

Pottery and porcelain wares made by Doulton and Company in Burslem, England, from the 1880s until 1903 were marked with the name *Doulton* in some form. Those marked *Royal Doulton* were made after 1903.

DURAND GLASS

This iridescent, American glass was produced at the Durand Art Glass Works, a division of Vineland Glass Works, in New Jersey from about 1924 until 1931. Much of it is signed *Durand.* Some pieces are numbered. Durand art glass is quite desirable.

ELFINWARE

Originally inexpensive porcelain pieces, Elfinware was made in Germany from about 1915 until the early 1940s. Raised flowers were a popular design. A variety of marks were used, including *Elfinware, Germany, Made in Germany*, and a crown with an *M.*

E. S. GERMANY AND E. S. PRUSSIA

From 1860 until 1925, the Erdmann Schlegelmilch factory in Suhl, Germany produced and sold both white ware and decorated porcelain. These pieces were marked *E. S. Germany.* At the same time, Erdmann Schlegelmilch's factory in Saxony, Prussia was making wares similar to those of its German counterpart. These were marked *E. S. Prussia.* Pieces marked *R. S. Germany* were produced by Erdmann's brother, Reinhold.

FLOW BLUE

Approximately ninety-five percent of all flow blue (also spelled flo blue) was made in the Staffordshire section of England. Flow Blue is characterized by a cobalt blue design that runs, or flows, into a white background. The more flowing or smudged the pattern, the more valuable the piece. Most pieces are backstamped with the name of the manufacturer, although these names are often difficult to read due to the effect of the flowing. Flow blue first enjoyed popularity in the 1820s. Oriental designs were often featured. Pieces decorated in gold are later than those without it.

FULPER

This pottery was in production in New Jersey from 1860 until 1930, when it became Stangl Pottery. The earlier pieces consisted of useful items such as stoneware bottles, jars, and churns; these are not readily found on today's market. You're more likely to spot some of Fulper's art pottery that they began making around 1910. Prized for the lovely glazes on these pieces, most are marked *Fulper, Rafco, Prang,* or *Flemington.*

GALLÉ, EMILE

Gallé was a Frenchman who made furniture, glass, and pottery in the art nouveau style from 1874 until 1904 when he died. His factory continued operating, making glass and furniture until 1931 when it closed. You may have to hunt for the name *Gallé,* as it was often incorporated into the design on a piece. Gallé glass is highly treasured.

GRUEBY

From 1897 until 1920, the Grueby Faience Company produced tiles, art pottery, and garden statuary. The factory, in Boston, Massachusetts, perfected a green matte glaze that became Grueby's hallmark until it was copied by several other art potters. Grueby's high quality wares are marked *Grueby Faience Co.; Grueby Pottery, USA;* or *Grueby, Boston, Mass.,* often in a circle with a flower inside.

HEISEY GLASS

From 1896 until 1957, in Newark, Ohio, A. H. Heisey and Company produced glass pieces in many designs and patterns. Beginning in 1901, Heisey marked items either with an *H* in a diamond, or with a paper label. The mark is often on the stem of a glass, near the spout of a pitcher, or hidden in some other manner. In 1960, three years after Heisey closed its doors, the Imperial Glass Corporation obtained the rights to some of the Heisey molds. From that time until 1968, Imperial Glass Corporation used the familiar *H* in a diamond mark.

INDIAN TREE

Used on china since the late 1800s, this pattern depicts a scene with flowers and the branch of a crooked tree. It's very colorful, incorporating an array of hues from orange through blue. China with older Indian Tree decorations are desirable, but the newer pieces aren't worth very much. Look for signs of wear.

KOCH PLATES

In the early 1900s, plates decorated with birds, animals, vegetables, and/or fruits were produced in Germany. The name *Koch* is signed on the front of these plates, making them easy to identify.

LALIQUE GLASS

In 1909 the talented designer René Lalique opened a glassworks in France. Produced of high quality, his lead-based glass objects were acclaimed throughout the world by 1930. Most of the perfume bottles, vases, plates, paperweights, statues, etc., are acid-etched. Lalique glass is still made today, but the pieces that are most highly prized are marked *R. Lalique,* or *R. Lalique, France* and were made before his death in 1945 at which time the *R* was dropped.

LIMOGES PORCELAIN

Limoges, France is the site of many porcelain factories because of the high quality of clay available there. From the mid-1800s until the present, all manner of items from dinnerware to vases and humidors to lamps have been created there. Each factory has its own marks, most of which incorporate the word *Limoges.* Often you'll find two marks—one from the factory where the white ware was made and another from the factory where the piece was decorated. Many Limoges items were sold as blanks and decorated by housewives and hobbyists. Pieces hand-painted in the factory are worth more than either transfer pieces or those decorated by an amateur. An artist's signature and date further enhance a piece. There are lists of Limoges marks that will acquaint you with the various dates when they were used.

LOCKE ART

This etched glass was made during the late 1800s and early 1900s by Joseph Locke in Pittsburgh, Pennsylvania. Most of his pieces are marked either *Joseph Locke, Jo Locke,* or *Locke Art.* You may have to hunt for the mark, as it was usually hidden in the pattern of the glass.

LUSTERWARE

Although lusterware has been made since the 1500s, the examples you're apt to run across at flea markets and auctions were produced from the late 1800s until the present. This shiny metallic finish comes in copper, silver, gold, and pink and is often used in combination with flowers, scenes, or geometric designs.

MAJOLICA

Much of this usually highly colorful pottery, which is glazed with a tin enamel, isn't marked. The Majolica that we know today and that you're liable to encounter at auctions, flea markets, and occasional garage sales dates from the mid-1800s through the 1930s, although some is still being made. It's safe for the novice to stick to pieces that bear the backstamps *Etruscan, Avalon,* or *Clifton*. You may find plates, pitchers, umbrella stands, tea sets, and a number of other items made from Majolica. The soft clay from which Majolica was fashioned made it quite vulnerable, and many of the older, more desirable pieces have a chip here or there. Majolica is one of the few categories of antiques in which a damaged piece is still quite valuable. Of course, a mint piece is better.

MARBLEHEAD POTTERY

This pottery was developed as occupational therapy for patients in a hospital in Marblehead, Massachusetts, around the turn of the century. The baskets, bowls, tiles, vases, etc., mostly decorated with marine designs, were so well accepted that within two years the pottery separated from the hospital. The factory continued until the mid-1930s when it was closed. Marblehead pottery is highly prized. It's marked with a stylized sailing ship flanked by an *M* and a *P* and enclosed in a circle.

MONMOUTH POTTERY

Cookie jars, vases, pitchers, dishes, and many other useful items were produced in Illinois by the Monmouth Pottery Company, starting in 1892. In 1906 the Western Stoneware Company incorporated Monmouth. The wares made before 1930 are sought. These mostly moderately priced items are marked with a maple leaf.

NEWCOMB POTTERY

This pottery, started by students at Newcomb College in New Orleans, Louisiana in the late 1800s, produced art pottery until the 1940s. Most pieces had a matte finish and an incised decoration. It is highly prized and easily recognizable by the initials *NC.* Many pieces were initialed by the artists who designed them.

NIPPON PORCELAIN

From 1891 until 1921, many Japanese companies marked their porcelain with the word *Nippon,* meaning Japan. This was used in conjunction with a great many other marks that identified the individual factories. Several forgeries of these marks have been found in recent years. The maple leaf mark and the rising sun mark are two that have been used on newer items. But the recent marks are easy to identify if you familiarize yourself with the original rising sun and maple leaf marks. After 1921, the word *Japan* replaced Nippon.

NORTHWOOD

With factories in Indiana, Pennsylvania, and Wheeling, West Virginia, Harry Northwood produced many types of glass from 1902 until his death in 1923 when his factories closed. Although the name Northwood is usually associated with carnival glass, the Harry Northwood Glass Company also produced goofus glass (a glass with the pattern embossed on the reverse side then painted, usually in gold and red) and custard glass (which was so named because its texture resembles that of the pudding). Many Northwood pieces are marked with an *N* that is underlined. This is easily seen by holding the article up to a light.

ORREFORS GLASS

While much of the Orrefors glass that surfaces at auctions and occasionally at flea markets is quite new, the Orrefors factory has produced high quality perfume bottles, plates, vases, etc., since 1898. This Swedish glass is heavy, sometimes etched, and is generally signed with the name *Orrefors.*

OYSTER PLATES

Produced by a number of manufacturers and varying greatly in quality, oyster plates were generally made to hold six oysters. These plates have indentations the size and shape of oysters. They were used extensively during the late 1880s when there was a special type of plate or receptacle for almost every food that was served.

PIRKENHAMMER

This porcelain, backstamped with the mark of two crossed hammers, was made in Bohemia during the early 1800s. The Pirkenhammer Company produced tablewares and lithopanes, usually decorated with either a scenic design or floral theme.

QUIMPER

Made in Quimper, France, in three factories, this tin-glazed pottery is hand-decorated and features flower and peasant designs. The mark usually includes the word *Quimper.* The earliest Quimper was known as HB Quimper and was first produced in 1685; Porquier was founded in 1772 and is marked with an *AP* or *P;* HR Quimper came along in 1778. By 1968 the three companies had merged, and in 1984 were sold to a United States firm that operates as Les Faïenceries de Quimper.

ROOKWOOD POTTERY

This very desirable art pottery is easily identified by a backstamp depicting a flame with a reverse *R* flanked by a *P*. Examples without numbers were produced from 1880 until 1900. Numbered pieces were made from 1900 until 1960. Some Rookwood molds have been used recently, but the items are clearly marked as reproductions.

ROYAL COPENHAGEN

Many items, including candlesticks, vases, and bowls, have been produced by this pottery, founded in Denmark in 1772. They are best known for the blue and white plates they produce annually and for their figurines. Pieces are marked with a crown over three wavy lines.

ROYAL CROWN DERBY PORCELAIN

Founded in the late 1800s, Royal Crown Derby porcelain was the first in a group of companies that now includes Worcester, Crown Derby, and Derby porcelains. Pieces made before 1921 will *not* have the words *Made in England* in the backstamp. The cups, dishes, pitchers, vases, etc., are marked with a crown and the company name.

SILESIA

Porcelain made at the Reinhold Schlegelmilch factory in Tillowitz, Germany, from about 1915 until 1935 is marked *R. S. Silesia.* Silesia was made by the same family that produced R. S. Germany and R. S. Prussia.

STEVENS AND WILLIAMS GLASS

Art glass, cameo glass, and etched glass were produced in Stourbridge, England, by the Stevens and Williams Company between 1830 and 1930. Intricately decorated pieces depicting works of nature such as flowers, trees, and leaves were the most popular. Many Stevens and Williams items are marked with an *S* and a *W.*

Furniture

While American-made furniture is more popular in most parts of this country than furniture made elsewhere, there is always a market for the better examples of any period, regardless of their origins. Much furniture has been reproduced, so it's important before making a purchase to arm yourself with as much knowledge as possible.

Insides of drawers that look suspiciously fresh or new wood on the back of furniture may mean that the piece is new or that the piece has been restored. Then again, further checking may reveal that most of the item in question is "right" (a term used to describe an item that *is* what it is touted to be). Old reproductions are valuable to the antiques dealer, but they should be purchased and sold for what they are.

Proceed with caution when you're buying a piece that is made in two sections, such as a bookcase or cupboard. Inspect both sections well to ascertain whether the pieces really go together or if they were "married" by someone along the way. The term "married" is used by antique dealers in referring to a piece that may be old but is comprised of sections from two different items. For instance, a dresser may be mated with a mirror from another dresser or the bottom of a sideboard may be fitted with a top that isn't the original one. There is little value in married furniture. What you have is two incomplete items.

The following is a list of the various furniture styles and some of their identifying marks. It won't give you all you need to know to be an expert, but it will give you a point from which to start—a bit of knowledge that you can build on. The table on pages 42–43 will give you an overview of styles and periods.

ADAMS

An architectural appearance featuring classical motifs painted by skilled artists identifies Adams furniture made in England from 1760 until 1793. The wood was generally mahogany and of a rectangular construction. Silk and other light, elegant fabrics were used for upholstery.

AMERICAN COUNTRY

Simple, rustic pieces made by rural cabinetmakers in the United States from 1690 until 1890, common American Country furniture included slat-back chairs, Boston rockers, trestle tables, dry sinks, wagon seats, and corner cupboards. Pine was commonly used to make American Country.

ANGLO-JAPANESE

Oriental-style furniture with bamboo-like turned legs and moldings was made in the United States from 1880 until 1910. Designs were asymmetrical and decorated with Oriental motifs. Many woods were used.

ART DECO

Chrome, glass, Bakelite, paint, lacquer, and veneer all went into producing art deco furniture with its streamlined, mechanized styling. While art nouveau lines were long and flowing, art deco lines were abrupt. Art deco was in vogue both in the United States and France from 1925 until 1945.

Furniture Styles
Period Produced and Country of Origin

Italian Renaissance	Italy	c. 1400–1700
Elizabethan	England	1558–1603
French Renaissance	France	1558–1625
Early Jacobean	England	1603–1660
Louis XIII	France	1610–1643
Colonial	United States	1625–1689
Louis XIV	France	1643–1715
Late Jacobean	England	1660–1688
Painted Italian	Italy	1680–1820
William and Mary	England	1689–1702
	United States	1700–1725
American Country	United States	1690–1890
United States Country	United States	1690–1890
Queen Anne	England	1702–1714
	United States	1725–1750
Regence	France	1715–1723
Louis XV	France	1723–1774
English Chippendale	England	1749–1779
United States Chippendale	United States	1755–1799
Adams	England	1760–1793
Louis XVI	France	1774–1789

Hepplewhite	England	1780–1795
Federal	United States	1790–1820
Shaker	United States	1790–1900
Directoire	France	1795–1799
Sheraton	England	1795–1810
Regency	England	1795–1830
French Empire	France	1805–1815
United States Empire	United States	1815–1840
Victorian	England United States	1830–1900 1830–1900
Cottage	United States	1860–1920
Anglo-Japanese	United States	1880–1910
Arts and Crafts	England United States	1890–1920 1890–1920
Colonial Revival	United States	1890–1925
Art Nouveau	United States France	1895–1914 1895–1914
Mission	United States	1890–1920
Depression	United States	1920–1942
Art Deco	United States France	1925–1945 1925–1945

Furniture

ART NOUVEAU

Flowing lines depicting natural subjects and incorporating swirls, girls with long luxurious hair, and curls of ivy, etc., marked the art nouveau period from 1895 until 1914 in both the United States and France. While many art nouveau items were popular in the United States, the furniture was appreciated by very few. The French, however, seemed enraptured with it. Many woods were used, including ash, walnut, and oak.

ARTS AND CRAFTS

A very popular movement from 1890 to 1920 in both England and the United States, the Arts and Crafts movement produced solid, simple, handcrafted furniture that displayed a medieval influence. It was usually made of oak. A slated construction was usually exposed as part of the design.

CHIPPENDALE, AMERICAN

Produced from 1755 to 1799, American Chippendale furniture featured either cabriole legs with ball or claw feet or straight, square legs. Chests and desks had bowed serpentine or oxbow fronts. This fine furniture was usually made of mahogany.

CHIPPENDALE, ENGLISH

Popular from 1749 until 1779, English Chippendale chairs, tables, and cabinets had carved aprons and skirts. Pieces were dark in finish and most had cabriole legs ending in ball and claw feet. The finest materials were used, and mahogany was often the wood of choice. Many pieces were japanned or decorated with marquetry mounted in gilded bronze.

COLONIAL

Often used to describe any furniture made in the United States prior to the Revolution, the term Colonial is used here to include only examples made from 1625 until 1689. Most Colonial furniture was made of oak and featured grooved stiles and rails. Carved panels were also commonly used.

COLONIAL REVIVAL

Much reproduction furniture mimicking the American Colonial style was produced in the United States from 1890 to 1925. Most of it was inferior and not true to the original, either in lines or quality. However, there was some fine furniture produced during this period that followed the Colonial style closely. Many woods were used.

COTTAGE

From 1860 until around 1920, inexpensive furniture made of pine was mass-produced in the United States. Lines were simple, and decorations were either painted or stenciled.

DEPRESSION

From 1920 until 1942, furniture manufacturers in the United States produced copies of earlier period styles. Most of these weren't fine quality, and few of them were authentic replicas of the furniture made during the period being copied. However, construction was solid. Veneers were often used as the finishing material. Cherry, mahogany, maple, and birch woods were commonly used.

DIRECTOIRE

These austere-looking pieces, usually made of mahogany, were produced in France from 1795 until 1799. Chairs either have backs that are concave or chair tops that curl toward the back. X supports were used. Often, chair arms were a continuation of the cylindrical, tapering front legs. Bas relief Greek and Roman designs were common.

ELIZABETHAN

Made in England from 1558 to 1603 and named for Elizabeth I, Elizabethan furniture features sturdy, extremely heavy rectangular lines and oak construction. The legs generally featured a large, carved ball. This was not fine furniture. It was extensively, if not expertly, carved.

EMPIRE, AMERICAN

From 1815 until 1840, furniture manufacturers in the United States copied the French Empire style.

EMPIRE, FRENCH

Made from 1805 to 1815, French Empire furniture was massive in appearance and very heavy to lift. It featured large, flat, plain surfaces sometimes adorned with marble. Thick legs curved forward in the front and backward in the back. Round tables had pedestal bases. Cherry was often used.

FEDERAL

A marriage of Hepplewhite and Sheraton designs dominated the Federal style, which was popular in the United States from 1790 until 1820. Ornamentation was often of a patriotic nature. Inlay, painting, and low relief carvings were often used. Most pieces were made of walnut or mahogany wood.

FRENCH RENAISSANCE

Heavily carved and large, French Renaissance furniture was made in France from 1558 to 1625. Oak was the wood of choice. The carving is better than that of the Elizabethan style, and the legs of pieces lack the carved ball.

HEPPLEWHITE

Small, graceful, straight-lined, with slender legs ending in small, spade feet or no feet were characteristic of this popular style made in England from 1780 until 1795. Shield-backed, oval-backed, or hoop-backed chairs were featured. Mahogany was the wood of choice; marquetry was used to make some pieces more elaborate.

ITALIAN RENAISSANCE

Made in Italy from about 1400 until 1700, Italian Renaissance is heavy, rectangular furniture. The dark walnut wood was massively carved in a variety of intricate designs. Upholstery was thick and luxurious.

JACOBEAN, EARLY

Made in England from 1603 until 1660, the Early Jacobean style of furniture is quite similar to Elizabethan but not as ornately carved. Made of oak, it was finished in a very dark stain.

JACOBEAN, LATE

Made from 1660 until 1688 (often referred to as the Restoration Period), this English furniture showed a strong influence of Italian baroque. It was made of walnut or oak, ornately decorated with scrolls, and featured lacquered ornamentation and gilt.

LOUIS XIII

Taken from Italian Renaissance styling, Louis XIII furniture was made in France from 1610 until 1643. Many pieces featured spiral legs fashioned from walnut wood. Chairs were low-backed.

LOUIS XIV

Rectangular structure and straight lines characterized this heavy furniture built in France from 1643 until 1715. Made of dark wood until late in the period when some lighter-colored woods were introduced, most pieces of Louis XIV furniture had underbraces and were so heavy that it was extremely difficult to move them.

LOUIS XV

Made in France from 1723 until 1774, Louis XV furniture was small, light, and highly decorated with inlay, gilding, polychroming, or artistic painting. Chests often had fronts that curved outward (known as bombé). Mahogany or walnut woods were used for this furniture.

LOUIS XVI

Smaller and more delicate than Louis XV, this French furniture was produced from 1774 until 1789 and featured straight, rectangular lines. Decorations were less detailed and pieces were often painted. The straight, tapered legs added to the fragile look.

MISSION

Catching onto the Arts and Crafts movement, from about 1890 to 1920, some United States furniture manufacturers produced oak furniture in that style. Although it was machine made, and Arts and Crafts was handmade, Mission was of fine quality.

PAINTED ITALIAN

Decorated with raised designs made of gesso, painted Italian furniture was made in Italy from 1680 until 1820. Cheap woods were often used but the pieces were beautifully painted, sometimes by some of the leading artists of the time. Legs and arms were curved. Many pieces had a bombé front.

QUEEN ANNE

Produced in England from 1702 until 1714 and in the United States from 1725 to 1750, much Queen Anne furniture had club feet or ball and claw feet. Its delicate curved lines usually ended in cabriole legs. Spoon chairs were popular, stretchers were not. Shell ornamentation was used extensively. The wood of choice was walnut, although cheaper wood was sometimes used and topped with a walnut veneer.

REGENCE

Produced in France from 1715 to 1723, the Regence style of furniture offered more curves and fewer rectangles on chair rails than previous styles. The pieces themselves were of a small size, and the rather small decorations were often made of ornamental metal.

REGENCY

Noted for its uncomfortable chairs, the Regency style was made in England from 1795 until 1830. The simple form and decoration were fashioned from rosewood, mahogany, or other fine woods. There was no carving, but brass was frequently used to create dolphins, swans, scrolls, and other fancy additions.

SHAKER

Simple, functional, maple or pine, and handmade, Shaker furniture was turned out in the United States from 1790 until sometime around 1900. It wasn't until after 1860 that it was sold to the secular market.

SHERATON

This English style mimics Hepplewhite in many ways, and was popular from 1795 until 1810. Proportions were pleasing to the eye and were lighter and more graceful than Hepplewhite. Turned legs were generally reeded or fluted, tapering to small, turned feet. Combinations of woods were used, but mahogany was most prevalent; veneers and inlays, common. Striped material was generally used for upholstery.

VICTORIAN

From 1830 until 1900, the Victorian period in England, furniture was made both there and in the United States in three styles—all are called Victorian. The best known is the large, decorative type made usually of oak with lots of carving and ornate gingerbread. A smaller, less decorative style was also produced. The third, and least known, Victorian furniture was large and undecorated. This was usually made of mahogany or rosewood and was often of a better quality than the first two styles, which were considered poor both in design and construction.

WILLIAM AND MARY

Made in England from 1689 to 1702 and in the United States from 1700 to 1725, William and Mary furniture featured turned legs, often in the shape of trumpets. X-shaped stretchers, often with ornate finials in the middle, were common as were hooded cabinets and large ball or bun feet. Several woods were used, including beech and walnut.

Miscellaneous Antiques

COFFEE GRINDERS

In use from the 1890s until the 1930s, box-shaped coffee grinders usually had handles on the top and deposited the ground coffee in a drawer at the bottom of the grinder. The larger coffee grinders that stand on the floor were used in stores and are considerably more difficult to find than the home variety.

GUTTA-PERCHA

An early plastic material made from tree resins, gutta-percha was used extensively to make the frame cases used to display daguerreotypes in the 1800s.

PHONOGRAPHS

Bringing music into the lives of millions, the phonograph made its debut in the 1880s. Examples with decorative horns are particularly desirable. Often the records that come with an old phonograph prove to be worth even more than the phonograph itself.

QUILTS

Made from the 1600s up to the present, quilts were originally handmade, usually from scraps of material left over from sewing projects. There are many designs and motifs. Look for hand stitching and clean examples. Don't bid on a quilt at auction unless both sides of it have been held up for examination. If possible, smell the material to ascertain that it isn't mildewed.

ROYCROFT

Leather articles, copper items, embroidery pieces, and jewelry were expertly hand-fashioned by the Roycrofters—followers of artist and writer Elbert Hubbard. Their community in Aurora, New York, flourished from the late 1800s until the early 1900s. The books, bookends, candlesticks, lamps, vases and many other articles they produced are marked with an *R* in a circle from which a symbol resembling a television antenna protrudes.

SNUFF BOXES

In the late 1700s and the early 1800s, ladies and gentlemen were fond of using snuff. It became fashionable to carry it in small receptacles made of gold, silver, enamel, and other materials. The material of a person's snuff box often indicated the class to which the individual belonged. Most snuff boxes were small, measuring an inch or two in length.

TEA CADDIES

In the 1700s, tea was so scarce that it was kept in locked boxes. These caddies were made of a variety of materials, from silver, copper, and brass to mahogany, fruitwood, and enameled wood. When tea became more abundant in the 1800s, caddies were still used, but they were no longer made with locks.

CHAPTER 3

Know Your Collectibles: An Indispensable Overview

What is a collectible? How does it differ from an antique? These questions aren't easily answered, because while some items definitely fall into the collectibles field and others can be only thought of as antiques, there's a gray area into which fall articles that are old or older and still are collected. Baseball cards, commemorative plates, Avon bottles, Hummel figurines, Disneyana, and salt and pepper shakers are a few examples of merchandise that anyone would place under the heading of collectibles. Articles from these categories can be as recent as last month or may go back several decades. People may look for anything that's ever been done in these categories, or they may collect just a special segment of what's available.

The United States Customs Office defines an antique as any object that's a minimum of 100 years old. However, Webster's Dictionary seems to take issue with the customs people. It says an antique is "a relic or object of ancient times or of an earlier period than the present." We tend to consider anything made prior to World War II as an antique. But this isn't a hard and fast rule. And collectibles and antiques may overlap. For instance, there are items—postcards, for example—that go back much further than World War II that we would put into the collectibles category. Most collectibles are mass-produced. Many popular examples surface in all of the markets. We find that having a good selection of collectibles along with antiques makes for a more interesting booth and increases our sales.

The collectibles field is a fickle one. What's in today may be out a month from now. Baseball cards, which in the past several years have enjoyed a rush of almost crazed enthusiasm, appear to be on the wane. Last year kids were buying and trading and expecting to pay for their college educations with the profits from their collections. This year only the older cards with notable players seem to draw any real interest. The problem, of course, is that baseball cards have little intrinsic value and are produced in huge numbers. Scarcity is always a determining factor in value.

Some collectibles have a strong, and what appears to be an ongoing, following. Salt and pepper shakers, postcards, and dolls, for instance, have a steady market. The current collectibles, those you see advertised in papers and magazines, in our opinion, are a risky investment. There are so many of them that interest on the secondary market is lukewarm. There are exceptions to this. Hummels, Rockwell plates, and some of the Precious Moments figurines are holding their value, and many are increasing annually.

We don't advise stocking up on any one collectible until you have become attuned to your market and know what your customers want. At that time, you may choose to select one or two collectibles as specialties, learning all there is to know about them. If you become an expert on a collectible that's popular in your area, collectors will come to rely on you as a source of merchandise. Regular customers are the backbone of the business. You'll be able to learn a great deal from the collectors as well. Most of them belong to clubs, and many of the clubs publish newsletters and hold meetings at which the latest information on their collectible is swapped by members. If you need advice on pricing or dating a collectible that you've purchased or want to purchase, these collectors' clubs are invaluable sources.

We've found that there's someone who collects almost anything. There are even collectors of moldy cheese. We advise sticking to the more conventional collectibles. You can wait a long time for a customer looking for the moldy cheese.

The following is a list of some collectibles you might want to look for in your search for merchandise. These are, in our opinion, items you're likely to find. There are many more types of collectibles that we don't mention, and because of the limitation of space, our descriptions are sketchy. There are entire books on most of these areas of collectibles.

ADVERTISING ITEMS

Ashtrays, boxes, booklets, buttons, mirrors, signs, paperweights, posters, bottle openers, trays, thermometers, trading cards, and a host of other items are collected because of the advertising that appears on them. A collector may hunt for examples from national companies or seek only items from a specific area. There are many reproductions of advertising items floating around in the markets. Most collectors look for examples dating from before the 1940s; those pieces from the late 1800s to the early 1900s are the most desirable.

AERONAUTICA

Baggage tags, airline dishes, playing cards—any memorabilia from, or to do with, any specific airline—are collectible. Items depicting, about, or from any of the various people who are well-known in the field of aeronautics, such as Charles Lindbergh or Amelia Earhart, are highly desirable. These may range from autographs, photographs, or biographies to medals, dolls, or candy containers.

ALUMINUM, HAMMERED

From the 1920s through the 1940s, decorative, as well as useful, hammered aluminum was popular. Pitchers, trays, tumblers, candy dishes, and any number of other items fashioned from this material graced American homes. It fell from favor after it was mass-produced to such an extent that it became common. Many of the old pieces are now being sought by collectors. This is a growing market.

AMERICAN DINNERWARE

The following companies made dinnerware that is now collected and that turns up often at garage sales, flea markets, and auctions. We find these wares to be brisk sellers: Blue Ridge; Crooksville China Company; Stangl; Taylor,

Smith, and Taylor; and Western Stoneware. All of these companies marked their products on the back.

ANIMAL TAGS

These tags are used to register animals. This isn't a category you'll be asked about every day, but if you find some examples that are very inexpensive, you might want to purchase them. Look for tags in the shapes of dogs, cats, and other animals. The tags should have a year on them, and those before 1930 are most sought. Many examples are made of metal, but during World War II, plastic and paper were used.

AUTOGRAPHS

Signatures of the famous and infamous surface from time to time. There are two things to consider in buying them. First, how common is the autograph? Second, how well known is the person? Entertainers, like Frank Sinatra, sign lots of pictures, menus, programs, etc., for fans. Often their signatures aren't worth as much as someone such as Orville Wright whose contact with the public wasn't as great. Authenticity is, of course, important.

AUTOMATA

Battery or key operated inanimate objects usually made of tin, tin and cloth, plush cloth over tin, or plastic have a strong collector following. The more complex the activity, the more desirable the piece. Condition is important to value, and having the box in which the object came is a big plus.

AVON

An assortment of soaps, perfumes, jewelry, plates, figurines, etc., made by the California Perfume Company and Avon Products, Inc., are found in large numbers at garage sales and flea markets. Collectors want items in mint or excellent condition. The original box is extremely important in this collectibles category. Bottles with product are preferred to those without, but this isn't as essential as the box.

BANKS

Both mechanical and still banks are desirable and have a strong market. Old cast-iron banks manufactured by Hubley Manufacturing, J&E Stevens, or A. C. Williams are quite valuable. A good paint job adds to the bank. Tin banks also are sought. Banks have been widely reproduced. Look for good-fitting seams; newer examples are usually inferior and fit together poorly.

BARBERSHOP COLLECTIBLES

Barbershop poles, chairs, basins, bottles, clocks, and signs have become so collectible that entire auctions have been dedicated to them. But if you're selling in a rural area, you could wait a long time to find a buyer for a barber chair. Meanwhile, it will take up a lot of space in your selling area. We advise sticking to smaller items in this category unless you're sure you have a buyer. Condition dictates price here.

BEATLES

There are avid Beatles fans out there who will pay you large sums of money for programs, photos, bubblegum cards, dolls, records, watches, and, in fact, anything old and original that features this band. Memorabilia will be more reasonably priced at a garage sale held by someone who has lost interest in a collection than at an auction or flea market where its value is common knowledge.

BEER BOTTLES AND CANS

Full-sized and miniature bottles are collectible. Older bottles are easy to spot since most had different closures than those used today. Beer cans should be clean, dent and scratch free, and have been opened from the bottom. Collectors generally seek examples of bottles and cans from breweries in the area in which they live. However, some people prefer to build collections with a national representation. We advise starting out with local examples.

BELLS

Another fairly stable collectible, bells of every type from limited edition collector bells to school bells, from sleigh bells to door bells, from glass bells to brass bells are desirable. Often bells can be purchased inexpensively at garage sales. Be sure the clapper, or whatever makes the bell function, is intact and that the bell rings well. Often clappers have been replaced, and the result is a bell that has little sound.

BIG LITTLE BOOKS

The most familiar Big Little Books are the three-and-five-eighths-inch by four-and-a-half-inch by one-and-a-half-inch editions initially published by the Whitman Publishing Company in the 1930s. They feature a myriad of subjects including cartoon characters, detectives, airplanes and flying, jungle escapades, movie stars, Western plots, and sports. Whitman tried several sizes before settling on the popular size. Other publishers have copied the format. Condition is important, but perfect examples are few.

BLACK MEMORABILIA

Advertising pieces, books, dolls, cookie jars, salt and pepper shakers, banks, games, doorstops, sewing items, magazines, etc., featuring African-Americans, are highly collectible. Many of these depict their subjects in less than flattering ways. Black memorabilia has been and is being widely reproduced especially in paper items, cast articles such as doorstops or banks, and salt and pepper shakers. As a result, this market has lessened a bit from what it was a few years ago.

BOTTLE OPENERS

Look for bottle openers featuring advertising, produced in figural shapes, or made as souvenirs from various places.

BRITISH ROYALS

Fascination with British Royals is almost as pervasive in the United States as it is in England and Canada. Inexpensive mementos from as far back as Queen Victoria's time were mass-produced to be given out to the royal subjects to commemorate auspicious occasions. These are sought by collectors, but there are also fine pieces made by companies such as Royal Doulton and Wedgwood, which because of their quality, command higher prices. Of course, the ill-fated marriage of Diana and Charles inspired an abundance of related collectibles. Some of these, depicting the happy couple, are quite reasonable and easy to obtain. Others, such as a limited edition set of cars bearing the royal couples' initials, sell in the thousands and are rare.

BUBBLEGUM CARDS

Many of the same companies that produce sport cards—Dunruss, Fleers, Bowman, Topps, etc.—put out bubblegum cards with nonsport subjects such as radio and television stars, space, military figures and happenings, and historic events. Try to buy them in complete sets rather than individually; you'll pay less. Cards should be in mint condition with no bent corners. Any damage greatly decreases the value.

BUTTONS

These are fairly inexpensive items that a large number of people collect. Look for interesting buttons in unusual designs. The bottles and baskets of buttons that come up at auction or surface at flea markets rarely contain any collectible buttons. There are four main divisions in button collecting: old, modern, uniform, and specialized. Old buttons, which date prior to the year 1918 and are the most collectible, are divided into 289 categories.

BUTTONHOOKS

Relics from the late 1800s and early 1900s, buttonhooks come in plain and fancy designs. Most of them are from ten to thirteen inches long. Though the hook part is fairly standard and not too interesting, the handles were fashioned in a variety of shapes from an assortment of expensive and inexpensive materials. Among the expensive materials are sterling, silver plate, ivory, mother-of-pearl, and jade. Some handles carry advertisements and are collectible on two levels—by the buttonhook collectors and the advertising collectors.

CALENDAR PLATES

There's no guesswork involved in dating this collectible. The first plates date from the late 1880s, but calendar plates from the early 1900s to the 1920s are easiest to find and most desirable. Many of these plates were advertising pieces given by merchants to their customers as Christmas gifts; most are marked, "Compliments of the Season." The main design is in the middle of the plate surrounded by a year of monthly calendar pages. The central design varies greatly, but trains, flowers, Gibson girls, notable people, and planes were popular themes.

CALENDARS

People collect old calendars for their designs. The most popular ones are advertising pieces.

CANDLEWICK

Glass objects with a trim of round glass beading were made by the Imperial Glass Corporation from 1936 until 1982. Although most of the pieces are plain crystal, Imperial did create light blue, cobalt blue, and red in the late 1930s and early 1940s. Imperial molds have been purchased by other companies, and candlewick has been copied extensively. The original Imperial candlewick is highly collectible with the colored pieces, which are hard to find, bringing the best price.

CANDY CONTAINERS

Most candy containers were made in Jeannette, Pennsylvania, by J. H. Millstein, T. H. Stough, or J. C. Crosetti companies. These glass, bisque, or paper holders were produced in a variety of shapes from airplanes, automobiles, and boats to dogs, cats, and roosters. The containers most sought by collectors are complete with the original pebble-like candies and still have the original seal. Containers that have been opened and are without product are still worth buying, but they don't command anywhere near the price of the unopened examples.

CANDY MOLDS

From about 1880 until the early 1940s, candy manufacturers presented their wares in a variety of impressive shapes. These were achieved with the use of candy molds. Some molds were used for chocolates, others for hard candies, and still others for maple sugar pieces. Look for molds with the place of origin marked on them—usually Germany, Holland, or New York—although unmarked molds are desirable. Rust or scratch marks greatly reduce the value of candy molds.

CANES

In the late 1800s and early 1900s, canes—gold, silver, wooden with decorative handles, and even glass—were an important fashion accessory for the well-dressed male. Both the material from which a cane is made and the elaborateness with which the handle is fashioned are considerations in determining value. Cane collectors look for the unusual.

CARTOON CHARACTERS

Most collectors favor characters from one particular cartoon strip. Peanuts characters are especially popular at this time, but there is also interest in Little Orphan Annie, Betty Boop, Li'l Abner, Garfield, and, of course, the Disney characters. These cartoon figures have been used to promote products and as illustrations in games, figurines, books, pictures, and a seemingly endless list of other products.

CATS

Our feline friends have gained in popularity over the past few years, and as a result items portraying them have increased in desirability. While older items such as advertising pieces, books, calendars, folk art, and so forth depicting cats are the most prized by collectors, newer articles sell fairly quickly to people who just like anything with a cat on it. Like many collectibles categories, this one overlaps others. Both cat collectors and Garfield collectors will purchase anything featuring Garfield. Railroad collectors will be enthusiastic about merchandise with Chessie the Chesapeake cat on it. A cookie jar collector will want at least one cat jar in a collection.

CHASE CHROME

During the 1930s, chrome items were all the rage. Cocktail shakers, smoking stands, lamps, pancake sets, napkin holders, warming trays—just to name a few—were manufactured in this material. The Chase Brass and Copper Company was a leader in production, and their deco-style wares are often seen at garage sales and flea markets. Avoid articles with rust, dents, or scratches. There are enough mint pieces available to make damaged ones almost unsalable.

CHILDREN'S DISHES

Akro Agate, metal, porcelain, and glass were all used to make delightful child-sized dishes. Sets are the most desirable, but individual pieces or incomplete sets are worth buying too. The original box adds to the value. Broken, cracked, or rusted pieces are worth little.

CIGAR BOXES

The most expensive cigar boxes were made of cedar, but all cigar boxes bearing colorful labels of the over 20,000 brands of cigars produced in the United States in the late

1800s and early 1900s are collectible. Embossed labels trimmed with gold are prized.

CIGAR FLAGS

Flannel flags found inside cigar boxes may depict flags of various nations or just feature a colorful design. These flags appear at auctions and flea markets, and while they're not "hot sellers," they do seem to have a core of collectors.

CIRCUS MEMORABILIA

Old ticket stubs, advertisements, and especially posters from the circus are avidly collected. With lithographed posters, look for the printer's identity in the margin. It should be clear and not blurred.

CLOWNS

Pictures of clowns, statues of clowns, and objects bearing the images of clowns all claim a strong circle of collectors. This collectible seems to stay fairly strong, not falling from favor as do some other collectibles.

COCA COLA

First sold in Atlanta, Georgia, in the mid-1880s, Coca Cola caught on fast, and by 1893 the syrup was available in all the states. However, it wasn't bottled until 1899. The word "coke" wasn't used until 1940. Any item with the Coca Cola name, whether it's a bottle, a sign, a tray, a plate, an old advertisement, or a mug, is collectible. Trays and advertisements featured such stars as Lillian Russell, Johnny Weissmuller, and Margaret Sullivan.

However, almost all Coca Cola items have been reproduced. If you're in doubt as to authenticity, it's best to pass up an article.

COLOGNE BOTTLES

Since most cologne bottles were made to be used in pairs, that's the way you want to buy them. Cologne bottles are slightly larger than the average perfume bottle. They were made by some of the leading glass companies, including Lalique. There are many milk glass cologne bottles on the market; most have worn, painted designs. We find these are difficult to sell because they are so common.

COMIC BOOKS

Scarcity rather than age dictates the value of this popular collectible. In fact, comic books printed before 1938 are worth almost nothing. Look for #1 issues, and be on the lookout for reprints that are often a different size from the original. While the comic book industry is booming today, we predict that it will not hold up. There is little actual value in these books, yet some of them are selling for thousands of dollars.

COOKBOOKS

Many of the collectible cookbooks were published by individual manufacturers and contain recipes featuring their products. With rare exceptions, these books and booklets are inexpensive, but we find them to be consistently good sellers. Most cookbooks issued after the 1970s are too new to evoke much interest from a collector. Don't purchase cookbooks unless their covers and pages are clean. Food stains are a real turnoff.

COOKIE CUTTERS

The most desirable cookie cutters are those that were skillfully handcrafted before the 1890s when manufacturers hopped on the cookie wagon and began producing cookie cutters. However, even these early, mass-produced examples are collectible. Look for examples in unusual shapes. There are many types of cookie cutters—some are advertising cutters, others depict comic or storybook characters. There are metal cutters and plastic cutters. There are cutters made in the United States and there are foreign cutters. Some collectors specialize in only one type.

COOKIE JARS

McCoy, Brush McCoy, Abington Pottery, and Shawnee are names to look for in cookie jars. Examine the jars carefully. Nicks and cracks detract greatly from their value.

CRACKER JACK PRIZES

Beginning in 1912, brothers F. W. and Louis Rueckheim began putting prizes in the boxes of candy-coated popcorn they manufactured. Today there are many avid collectors seeking these tiny toys, which have been made of plastic since 1948.

CUPS AND SAUCERS

Bone tea cups and saucers are a good staple item. People have collected them for many years, although they aren't as high on the list of hot sellers as they were in the days when ladies served afternoon tea to their friends. Any damage to either component renders the set undesirable. Collectors look for examples they don't have, and we've found that cups with designs inside as well as outside are fast sellers.

DEGENHART GLASS

Between 1947 and 1978, John and Elizabeth Degenhart operated the Crystal Art Glass Company in Cambridge, Ohio. There they made pressed glass novelties and paperweights—figurines, toothpick holders, animal dishes, and other glass pieces—in a wide spectrum of colors. Today these are prized collectibles. A *D* in a heart identifies Degenhart Glass from 1972 until 1978. Prior to that, some pieces were marked with just a *D*. This glass has been reproduced in quantity.

DEPRESSION GLASS

Inexpensive glass dinnerware and other items made in many colors and a variety of patterns during the 1920s and 1930s are popular to collect. However, Depression glass has been widely reproduced, and interest in it isn't as strong as it was a few years ago.

DICK TRACY

A few years ago when the movie about this sleuth from the comic pages came out there was suddenly a great deal of merchandise on the market depicting Dick and his pals. Older merchandise doubled or tripled in price almost overnight. But the excitement has died down, and while Dick Tracy is still collectible, prices have dropped drastically.

DIONNE QUINTUPLET MEMORABILIA

Annette, Cecile, Emilie, Marie, and Yvonne Dionne were born in Ontario, Canada, on May 28, 1934. The first quintuplets ever to survive, their every move became newsworthy. Businesses with an eye for profit produced calendars, books, paper dolls, spoons, games, fans, and a wide selection of other merchandise depicting the five children who had captured the public's heart. Madame Alexander produced dolls in several sizes. Dionne quintuplet items are still in demand by collectors.

DISNEYANA

Mickey, Minnie, Donald Duck, and their cohorts as well as other Disney characters show up in all markets and in a variety of forms. Condition, age, and scarcity are key factors to a collector. Examples from the 1930s are the most desirable. Disney characters appear on banks, in books, as dolls, in comics, as paper dolls, on clocks, as figurines, etc.

DOG COLLECTIBLES

Small dogs, big dogs, mutts, and purebreds in all forms from figurines to doorstops, from planters to cookie cutters and jewelry are solid sellers. People often look for examples of their favorite breeds or items that look like a dog they own. While quality is a factor in determining price, it has little to do with salability. The poorest piece will sell if it strikes a collector's fancy.

DOOR KNOCKERS

Brass, cast iron, copper, and wrought iron are the main materials from which door knockers are made. They've been created in numerous shapes, including animals, hands, anchors, and ropes. The more unusual the knocker, the more desirable it is to a collector. The Coalbrookdale Company of England was the best known early manufacturer of door knockers.

DR. PEPPER

This caffeine-free soft drink dates from 1886. A strong advertising and promotional campaign made it a national favorite. These ad pieces are collectible. Early logos were in script. The period was dropped from *Dr.* in 1950.

DOLLHOUSE FURNITURE

Everything, including the kitchen sink, has been reproduced in miniature for use in dollhouses. The older examples are most desirable when they're in their original boxes with no missing pieces. Newer dollhouse furnishings have been made in minute detail and are also collectible.

DOLLS, MODERN

By far the most collectible of the modern dolls is Mattel's Barbie. The older dolls command high prices if they're in mint condition and in the original box. The absence of the box reduces the value by fifty percent. Barbie's clothes are also collectible if they're by Mattel and are in mint or excellent condition. Homemade clothing made by dedicated mothers and grandmothers has little market value. Ken, Midge, Skipper, and Barbie's other friends are also in demand. Cabbage Patch Dolls are another modern collectible. Xavier Roberts's originals are worth far more than those made by other companies. Madame Alexander, Nancy Ann Storybook Dolls, and Vogue Dolls are a few of the fairly modern dolls worth seeking.

DOLLS, OLD

Damage to old dolls reduces their value greatly. If it's extensive enough, it renders them noncollectible. Sleep eyes should open and shut easily; hair should be original and uncut; composition heads and limbs should be intact and not cracked; all dolls, except bisque dolls, should be in original clothing. It's also acceptable for a bisque doll to have replacement hair. Some of the most desirable dolls are those made by Armand Marseille, Belton, Effanbee, Kestner, American Character Doll Company (newer, but still not modern), and older Horsman dolls.

ELEPHANTS

Anything featuring an elephant is collectible. Some collectors concentrate on one category such as banks, figurines, or advertising material, while other collectors will buy anything with an elephant on it. Many people want only pieces with the elephant's trunk up, a symbol of good luck.

FANS

Everyone seems to be intrigued by a fan, especially on a hot summer's day. We've never had a fan, no matter how modern, that hasn't sold quite quickly. But the fine old fans are treasures. A few things identify them. Fans made before the mid-1800s didn't bear signatures and were never made from satin. There were no finger loops at the rivet by which to hold the fan. Among the fans sought by collectors are those with advertising; fans made of feathers; exquisitely painted European fans; very feminine lace fans; Oriental fans; and those made with sequins, especially the older sequins that can be identified by a seam where sections are joined—newer sequins are one piece.

FAST FOOD PREMIUMS

A new, and rapidly growing field of collectibles, fast food premiums include glasses, dolls, calendars, games, puzzles, combs, stickers—the list goes on and on. McDonald's memorabilia is the most popular, but Burger King, Dairy Queen, and Wendy's aren't far behind. This area of collectibles is inexpensive and, therefore, a good one for the beginning dealer to stock. But, as with most collectibles, we don't advise buying more than a few pieces unless you know you have a ready buyer.

FELIX THE CAT

First introduced in an animated cartoon in 1917, Felix was the creation of Paul Sullivan. Felix became a popular cartoon character of King Features Syndicate in 1923. He rose in status to a kind of superhero, and many products were made in his image, including dolls, which are particularly collectible. The comic strip continued until Sullivan's death in 1933.

FENTON GLASS

One of the leading manufacturers of carnival glass, Fenton is still made today. The factory also produced quality reproductions of early stretch glass, custard glass, and opalescent glass pieces. These are also collectible.

FIESTA WARE

A colorful dinnerware first made in 1936 by the Homer Laughlin China Company, Fiesta Ware is easily identified by concentric circles around the edges and in the centers of plates, saucers, platters, etc. In 1969 the ware was redesigned, new colors were added, and handles changed from full circles to partial circles. This dinnerware was discontinued in 1972. Many people collect Fiesta. In the 1980s a new Fiesta was introduced. It has little value as a collectible at present.

FIREHOUSE MEMORABILIA

Firemen, firemen's families, and insurance people are just a few of the people who collect items in this field. Look for badges, banners, buckets, match holders, cards, helmets, and fire extinguishers—anything pertaining to the firefighter. Old items such as a helmet will sell for far more than the newer ones. But be aware that the date on a helmet is probably the date the fire company started rather than the date the helmet was manufactured or used.

FISHING COLLECTIBLES

Old split-bamboo rods, plugs, and reels are the most sought collectibles in this growing field. But creels, nets, fly boxes, etc., are also desirable. Look for examples in good condition with original paint. These often surface at garage sales where people, unaware of the value, are eager to get rid of articles they don't use anymore.

FLAGS, AMERICAN

Some collectors will buy anything with the flag of the United States of America on it. Some people only purchase early flags with seven stars, thirty-six stars, forty-two stars, forty-five stars, or forty-eight stars. But many collectors seek anything that has a United States flag on it. This is an easy category to buy, because there is so much material. The thing to remember is that the more prominent the flag, the more valuable the piece is to a flag collector.

FOUNTAIN PENS

Eversharp, Parker, Sheaffer, and Waterman are all names to look for in fountain pens. Pens from the 1920s to the 1940s with self-filling lever action are desirable. Condition is very important, but you may sell a damaged pen to a collector who is looking for replacement parts. Pens with gold nibs (points) are more valuable.

FRANKART

These green metal, art deco accessories made in the 1920s and 1930s were known as "greenies." Products included lamps, art objects, vases, ashtrays, etc., and featured figures, many of them nudes. Frankart is marked with the company name along with the year each piece was manufactured. It is very desirable and brings a good price. The company also produced pieces with black or gray finishes.

FRANKOMA

Still produced today, the most collectible pieces of Frankoma were made prior to 1938 when the factory burned; it was subsequently rebuilt. These highly sought items are marked with the name *Frankoma* underneath the figure of a leopard.

FRATERNAL MEMORABILIA

All types of memorabilia from the various fraternal organizations is collected. Age and degree of ornamentation are very important. There are three types of collectibles within this category: personal possessions of individual members, including aprons, costumes, pins, badges, hats, and so forth; souvenir items from the many national and regional conventions held by an organization;

and furniture and other trappings from local halls owned by the organizations.

FRUIT CRATE LABELS

From the 1880s until the 1940s, most fruit was packed and shipped in crates. These crates bore colorful labels depicting everything from love scenes to Indians; all incorporated pictures of the fruit in question. The earliest labels were engraved, but lithographed labels were introduced by the 1930s. Look for labels in good condition. These are inexpensive collectibles.

FRUIT JARS

Collectors may seek jars from one region, jars of one color, jars that all have the same patent date, jars with a special type of closure, or any and all types of canning jars. Available at most flea markets and often found at garage sales, these jars date back to the early 1800s. Some are worth hundreds of dollars. Value can be ascertained only by studying this vast area of collectibles. Old fruit jars have been reproduced.

GAMES

Older board games have found a home among collectors and can often be found for a dollar or less at flea markets or garage sales. Occasionally a whole box of games will sell at auction for almost nothing. Those based on television or radio programs are popular. Look for boxes in good condition and games with all the pieces and instructions intact.

GEORGE AND MARTHA WASHINGTON PITCHERS

Made by the Homer Laughlin Company and originally sold for fifty cents at the 1939 World's Fair, George and Martha Washington pitchers are five-inches tall and depict their namesakes. They're hard to find, easy to sell, and worth over 100 times their original price.

GOLF COLLECTIBLES

One of America's favorite pastimes has inspired this field of collectibles. However, only old examples are truly valuable. The period from 1850 to 1895 is the one on which most collectors concentrate. Pieces before that are difficult to impossible to find, and those made after 1895 are too common to interest all but the novice collector. Bags, balls, and clubs are all sought as well as prints and pictures depicting the sport.

GONE WITH THE WIND COLLECTIBLES

The book itself, paper dolls, movie posters, and any items associated with this classic film are collectible. In 1991, the publication of *Scarlett* (the sequel to *Gone with the Wind*) created renewed enthusiasm.

GOOFUS GLASS

Known by a variety of names including "pickle glass," "hooligan glass," and "Mexican glass," goofus glass was originally produced as premiums and distributed at fairs and carnivals from 1890 to 1920. Most pieces were embossed and decorated on the underside of the glass. Carnations, strawberries, grapes, sunflowers, and peacocks were a few of the popular designs. Gold was a dominant color and was often accompanied by red, green, pink, or purple. Pieces with peeling paint are worth about half the value of perfect examples. Gold paint that has tarnished over the years often brightens with the gentle application of a fine metal polish.

GRANITEWARE

This enamel-coated iron or steel cookware was first made in Germany in the 1830s. Production started in the United States in the 1860s. Old graniteware is heavier than the newer type. A cast-iron handle dates a piece between 1870 and the turn of the century when wooden handles gained favor; these were used until 1910. Although white and gray are the most common colors, graniteware was also produced in blue, red, green, brown, yellow, and violet. Condition is important, but a bit of chipping in an old piece is acceptable.

HALL CHINA

Made as premiums for the Jewel Tea Company, Hall China Company teapots, bowls, cake plates, etc., were made from the 1920s to the 1950s and are marked on the bottom of each piece with the Hall China Company name. Autumn Leaf is the best known pattern in this china. Hall pieces are common and very salable.

HAT PINS

From the mid-1800s until about 1930 women secured their hats with the help of hat pins. Modest hat pins with plain simulated pearl heads are of little value, but the fancy, often jeweled, hat pins that adorned the headgear of elegant ladies are treasured by many collectors. Look for decorative heads with no missing or damaged parts or stones. The shanks should be straight and free of rust.

HAT PIN HOLDERS

Collectors of hat pins display their collections in hat pin holders. Collectible in their own right, these cylindrical vessels have holes in the tops into which the pins slide. They were made by many manufacturers. Some holders are very ornate and others quite plain. Many are hand-painted, either in the factory or by a consumer. But beware, they are being reproduced.

HOLD-TO-LIGHT POSTCARDS

These novelty postcards, with windows through which light shines, were made around the turn of the century. A church design was a common theme, although other buildings with windows were also used.

HORSE COLLECTIBLES

Cat lovers collect cat items, dog lovers seek anything depicting a dog, and horse lovers look for examples of the object of their affections. Some collectors seek old sleigh bells, bridles, currycombs, hitching posts, spurs, stirrups, and other equipment. Other horse people want figurines, bookends, cookie jars, pillows, prints, or any other items featuring horses.

HOT AIR BALLOON COLLECTIBLES

Balloon stamps and medals, engravings, posters, books, etc., have become collectible in recent years as the interest in hot air balloons has grown. Examples need not be old and are relatively inexpensive.

HULL POTTERY

The art pottery vases, ewers, sugar bowls and creamers, etc., are the pieces of Hull sought most by collectors. A matte finish means that a piece was made between 1930 and 1950. The factory burned down in 1950, reopening in 1952. A variety of articles, including cookie jars, planters, piggy banks, and dinnerware were made in a glossy finish until the plant closed in 1986. Some pieces are marked *Hull USA, Hull Art USA,* or *Hull.* Paper labels were sometimes used. Hull Pottery is a strong seller.

HUMMEL

Of the many figurines, plates, plaques, bells, Christmas ornaments, bookends, and dolls produced by the F. W. Goebel Company of Germany, the figurines are the most popular collectible. Condition, subject, size, and the mark on each Hummel all help to determine value. The crown mark that shows a crown with a stylized *WG* under it was used from 1934 until 1950. The full bee mark has a large bee (the insect) appearing in a *V* with part of the body and wings rising above the *V.* This mark was used from 1940 to 1956. These two marks are the oldest and most desirable. The "small bee" mark, the "high bee" mark, the "baby bee" mark, the "vee bee" mark, the "large stylized bee," the "small stylized bee," the "three-line" mark, the "last bee," and the "missing bee" followed in that order. The larger a figurine, the more valuable it is.

INKWELLS

The period between the early 1800s and the 1920s was the heyday of inkwells. Most liners were made of glass or pottery since these two materials are impervious to ink. Ornate inkwells in good condition bring good money. Lids were often replaced, so you must examine any inkwell to make sure it has the original one. A replacement lid greatly devalues the piece. A minor chip here or there inside the well or on the lid detracts only minimally from its value.

INSULATORS

In 1844 the first insulator designed for telegraph lines was patented. Since that time insulators have been made in over 500 styles, in a variety of colors, by several manufacturers. Those made prior to the Civil War were not threaded. Most insulators you'll see at flea markets or garage sales are very common. At this time there seem to be few collectors.

KEWPIES

A creation of Rose O'Neill in the early 1900s, the Kewpie doll won the heart of the public. With a pointed topknot and tiny wings, Kewpies were depicted on bells, calendars, postcards, clocks, and any number of other articles. Many a child went to sleep clutching a soft kewpie doll. Look for examples in good condition.

KEYS

These everyday items are collectible not so much for their value but for the symbolism attached to them. Keys have had a mystical appeal since Biblical times and were considered status symbols during the middle ages when people of noble birth carried them hanging from their garments. Modern keys are of little value to collectors who look for older keys and generally collect keys in one specific category such as car keys, desk keys, brass keys, railroad keys, door keys, etc. For the most part, keys are an inexpensive collectible.

KITCHEN COLLECTIBLES

Waffle irons, toasters, blenders, meat grinders, cherry pitters, apple peelers, rolling pins, and a host of small kitchen gadgets from days gone by are all collected. Some are put to use and others serve to create ambience in a kitchen. Appliances should be in working order and be at least thirty years old to have any appeal to the collector. Articles with painted wooden handles are desirable; peeling paint greatly lessens the value.

LETTER OPENERS

Letter openers made prior to 1935 are prized, especially those bearing an advertising message. They may be made of silver, celluloid, tin, or brass. Some people specialize. For instance, they may collect only openers depicting animals, or military subjects, or souvenir openers.

LIMITED EDITION COLLECTIBLES

Our advice on this vast field of collectibles is to tread cautiously. The media is full of advertisements for new limited edition items that are supposed to appreciate at an astronomical rate over the next few years. The trouble is that only a few of them actually go up in value. The rest either stay the same or depreciate. Bells, figurines, cups, Christmas ornaments, music boxes, dolls, plates, and cottages glut the market. We only purchase Norman Rockwell, Bing and Grondahl, Royal Copenhagen, or Knowles plates. Although they list high, we usually sit with them for awhile before a collector comes along. Precious Moments figurines are also worth purchasing if you can obtain them at a modest price.

LITHOPANES

These porcelain transparencies are hidden in a variety of objects and are revealed only when the object is held to the light. Lithopane pictures were used in tea cups, on lampshades, in coffee mugs, and other items that lend themselves to this type of decoration. Most were produced in the nineteenth century. Many were beautifully done by fine companies such as Meissen and Wedgwood. Less expensive lithopanes were created by many Oriental potters.

LUNCH BOXES

Who'd ever have thought that the lunch boxes that kids took to school would be collectible. And some command hefty prices considering what they cost originally. If the box isn't complete with the original thermos, the value is considerably less. The box should be free of rust and scratches and the decoration should be bright, not faded. Handles should be unbroken. The Beatles, superheroes such as Batman, TV programs including "The Beverly Hillbillies," and personalities such as the Osmonds are examples of themes that collectors seek.

MAGAZINE COVERS

Illustrated covers from old magazines have some collector value provided they're artist-signed and in good condition, the label doesn't interfere with the art, and they're neither faded nor musty.

MAGAZINES

Covers, advertisements, illustrations, and the subject matter of articles are all reasons why people collect magazines. Look for clean, unmusty examples published prior to 1960. Magazines from the 1930s and 1940s dealing with World War II are very popular. Those featuring the Vietnam War are gaining in collectibility. *Life* and *National Geographic* are two of the most popular magazine collectibles.

MARBLES

Size, type, and condition of marbles determine their value. Old, handmade glass marbles and novelty marbles, which may be newer, are considered the most collectible. Agates, clambroths, goldstones, steelies, and sulphides are a few types of marbles. Large marbles are worth more than small marbles, but size should only be a consideration when comparing marbles of the same type.

MCKEE GLASS

A fine glassware first produced by J. and F. McKee in 1850, the name of the company was changed to McKee and Brother in 1852, and ultimately to McKee and Brothers when another brother joined the firm in 1865. Pieces marked *pres-cut* or *McK* are particularly desirable to collectors, although most people will find a spot in their collections for any piece of McKee glass.

MILK GLASS

Many useful items were produced in milk glass—goblets, vases, fruit dishes, and "chicken on a nest" covered dishes, to name a few—and with years of use the sharp edges from the molds became smooth. Reproductions abound on the market, so beware. Look for examples marked with a patent date or number and preferably a signature. This is not a guarantee of authenticity, but it helps. The oldest pieces were made in white only. Straw marks, which were left by an obsolete firing process, mean a piece of glass, including milk glass, is old.

MORIAGE

Made by Japanese artisans, pottery pieces featuring applied clay relief designs are always salable. Vases, teapots, cups and saucers, urns, and many other objects were decorated in this manner, which involves slip trailing clay over the formed piece and using a stipling method to produce dots. Moriage pottery can also be made by forming strings of clay by hand and then applying them to the object.

MOVIE MEMORABILIA

Posters, lobby cards, brochures, sheet music, souvenirs, records or sound tracks, scripts, books, magazines, toys—in fact, anything that has to do with a hit movie—are highly collectible. Some collectors want only those things depicting a little-known movie, but you can wait a long time for one of these collectors to come into your booth. It's best to stick with the all-time greats such as *Gone with the Wind, Casablanca,* and *For Whom the Bell Tolls.*

MOVIE STARS

Many movie stars of yesteryear have become cult heroes, and any piece of merchandise dealing with them is collectible. This includes movie magazines, posters, pictures, dolls, paper dolls, coloring books, and a host of other products. Most collectors concentrate on one personality. The most popular include Marilyn Monroe, Humphrey Bogart, Clark Gable, Charlie Chaplin, Jean Harlow, and W. C. Fields.

MOXIE

This bitter tasting soft drink was popular from the mid-1880s to the 1940s, although it's heyday was from 1920 to 1940. Collectible items include tip trays, trays, glasses, bottles, ashtrays, tin signs, posters, dishes, etc. The rule of thumb is the older the piece, the more value it has to a collector. There are some exceptions to this. For instance, any piece featuring Ted Williams is held in high esteem.

MUFFINEERS

Shakers for sugar or a combination of sugar and cinnamon were standard household items during the 1800s. The wealth of the family dictated the ornateness of the shaker. Beautiful silver examples, cut glass shakers, and plain pieces of either clear or colored glass were produced. Muffineers are about three times the size of the standard salt shaker and have larger holes in the tops.

MUSIC BOXES

Lovely, expensive music boxes and small decorative boxes made today are collectible. The older boxes are too costly for the average collector to buy or for the average dealer to handle. Newer boxes are chosen either for their tunes or their design. For instance, one collector may only want boxes depicting animals while another collector may look for boxes that play themes from movies. These are good items to carry because they also appeal to people who aren't collectors.

NAPKIN RINGS

Although napkin rings graced American tables starting in the mid-1800s, it wasn't until much later in the century that figural napkin rings were made. Originally designed for children, these examples have become collectible among adults who often use them when they entertain. Old napkin rings made of celluloid, silver, bronze, bone, china, cloisonne, cut glass, and tin are also sought by collectors. Condition is important. A monogram greatly reduces the value.

NEW MARTINSVILLE GLASS

This glass company, founded in Ohio around the turn of the century, originally produced restaurant glasses and lamps but shortly after began making art glass objects in a variety of colors. After 1935 all colors except blue, crystal, pink, and ruby were discontinued. The earlier pieces are the most desirable to a collector. Objects were marked with a paper label. In the early 1940s, New Martinsville Glass Company became Viking Glass Company. Viking is still in business today.

NEWSPAPERS

Look for old papers in excellent condition. Those that herald some historic happening are most sought. The front page is the most important part of the paper to collectors. Many frame these pages and display them on walls.

NORITAKE AZALEA PATTERN

This pattern features pink azaleas and was made in Japan from about 1916 to 1940 exclusively for the Larkin Company, who used the pieces as premiums. There are several marks in several colors that denote the period during which the piece was manufactured, but collectors tend to mix periods. The more vivid the pink, the more desirable the piece. All types of dinnerware were produced in this pattern.

NUTCRACKERS

The most desirable modern examples of this collectible depict military figures and were made in former East Germany. Older nutcrackers made in the art deco and art nouveau styles are also popular with collectors. Look for signs of wear that indicate the nutcracker is old and actually was put to use rather than displayed as an ornamental reproduction.

NUTTING, WALLACE

A Jack of many trades, this multi-talented man was a furniture maker, photographer, publisher, and preacher. Though his furniture is reproduction, it is treasured today as are his books. *The Furniture Treasury,* his best known book, is one of the most respected references on American furniture. Wallace Nutting is well known for prints of the photographs he took of places he loved. His indoor shots are more precious than those taken of country lanes and pastures, but any signed Wallace Nutting print has a value that seems to increase yearly.

OCCUPIED JAPAN

Between 1945 and 1952 many items from figurines and tea sets to toys and metal objects of varying quality and value were produced in Japan for export. All are marked *Occupied Japan* or *Made in Occupied Japan.* Marks are underglaze; any that are overglaze are fake marks added to give a piece worth. These articles are sought by collectors because the items are easily dated.

OWLS

The wise old owl has been portrayed in figurines, on buttons, on posters, in pictures, on tape measure holders, glasses, mugs, advertising pieces, and almost anything else you can imagine. Because of this, any owl object that you buy may be desirable not only to owl collectors, but also to people who collect the object on which the owl is represented.

PADLOCKS

Simple padlocks as well as those with complicated workings are collected. Brass and iron are the most sought materials. Company names should be embossed, rather than stamped, on the padlock. Many, many different padlocks were made. In fact, one single company might have produced hundreds of designs, so this is an easy collectible to acquire. Don't buy examples that have been repaired, repainted, or are damaged in any way.

PAPER CLIPS

Not the ordinary paper clips of today, but the early spring-loaded paper clips, which were first used around

1850, have gained the attention of collectors. Made of sterling, silver plate, copper, brass, and even gold, these office helpers weren't thrown away. They were made in fanciful designs such as hands that clasped the papers together; an animal's head with a mouth that closed around whatever was to be kept together; or a duck whose beak could accommodate papers. By the start of World War I manufacturers turned to more essential items, and ornamental paper clips became a thing of the past. The more ornate a clip, the more its value.

PAPER DOLLS

Although most collectors of paper dolls look for uncut books or sheets rather than just one doll, cut sets are sought by some people. They will, however, bring far less than uncut sets. Two of the most valuable paper doll sets that we know of are Gone with the Wind from the 1940s and Quintuplets/The Dionne Babies, with a 1935 copyright.

PATRIOTIC MEMORABILIA

Some people look for anything featuring the Statue of Liberty, others search for eagles, still other collectors want only items depicting Uncle Sam. The Liberty Bell is popular too. While a few individuals will purchase any patriotic item, most people specialize in just one subject.

PHOENIX BIRD PATTERN CHINA

The mythological bird that rose from the ashes decorates this popular blue and white ware. Executed with varying degrees of expertise, many variations are available. Pheonix Bird was made in Japan starting around 1900.

PIANO BABIES

Bisque replicas of babies in various postures and dressed in everything from the height of baby fashion to not dressed at all graced piano tops in the late 1800s. They were created in all sizes from miniatures to life-size. One purpose they were supposed to serve was amusing small children while they practiced their piano lessons. Old piano babies are very desirable, but unfortunately you must beware of reproductions.

PIGS

Another animal collectible that has quite a following, pigs appear as cookie jars, figurines, salt and pepper shakers, stuffed animals, banks, in advertising, etc. Some of the most desirable pig collectibles are bisque figures made in Germany, but they've been extensively reproduced.

PINCUSHION DOLLS

Figures from the waist up, usually of women, were attached to pincushions. Generally, these figures were made of bisque or a glazed china. Few of the cushions have survived in good condition, but many of the figures can be found.

PLANTERS PEANUTS

The familiar Mr. Peanut logo adorns many advertising and promotional pieces put out by Planters Peanuts.

Founded in Wilkes-Barre, Pennsylvania in 1906, the company moved to Suffolk, Virginia in 1916. It was after this that the logo came into use. Early, Wilkes-Barre pieces are marked *Planters Nut and Chocolate Company.* Collectibles include salt and peppers, peanut grinders, nut sets, paperweights, jars, yo-yos, and may other plastic, tin, papier mâché, and ceramic articles.

PLAYING CARDS

Many themes are subjects for the designs on playing cards, from political conventions, fraternal organizations, World's Fairs, airline giveaways, and so forth, to animals, children, trains, ships, and exotic dancers. Topics are almost limitless. Collectors look for complete decks in the original boxes and in good condition.

POCKET KNIVES

Alca, Aerial, Canton, Case, Colonial, Golden Rule, Ka-Bar, Novelty Cutlery, Queen, Remington, Schrade, and Winchester are the major makers of collectible knives. Some collectors want strictly utilitarian knives, some buy knives for the designs, still others look for examples that were made for advertising purposes.

POLITICAL MEMORABILIA

Buttons, canes, banners, bumper stickers, posters, tokens, bandannas, flags, etc. from bygone elections are fairly strong, though not usually expensive, collectibles. Kennedy material is still produced; the newer Kennedy material is not desirable to a collector.

POSTCARDS

First used in the late 1860s, postcards enjoyed their greatest popularity from 1898 until about 1920. Produced in large numbers, cards from this time period are readily available. Many collectors seek examples with pictures of one particular city or state. Postcards with a geographical reference generally sell best in the area they depict. Select cards that are in excellent condition, and display them in plastic sleeves to avoid wear.

PRESLEY, ELVIS

"The King" has a large and devoted following ready to scoop up any Elvis item, including calendars, plates, autographs, music boxes, posters, postcards, records, scarves, etc. Look for a copyright that appears on all official Elvis memorabilia.

PUZZLES, JIGSAW

Look for old puzzles, many of which didn't have interlocking pieces. Collectors want clean, complete puzzles without must or mildew. Many people won't buy a puzzle unless it's displayed in assembled form. This can be done in a shadow box. But don't glue the puzzle to a base. Most collectors look for theme puzzles such as transportation, advertising, or personalities. Hand-cut puzzles are more desirable than machine-cut examples.

RADIOS

Collectors look for radios made before World War II. The 1920s produced battery-powered receivers, crystal sets, and electric table radios. By the 1930s consoles had been added as had plastic portables and table models with wooden cabinets. The scarcity of a model dictates the price and desirability. Condition is very important. A radio that works will bring twice as much as one that doesn't. Anything but very minor scratching of the cabinet greatly reduces the value.

RAILROAD MEMORABILIA

The glamour of the railroads beckons collectors who seek ashtrays, lanterns, china, brochures, watches, badges, and anything that bears the logo of a railroad. Collectors usually want items from railroads local to them. Pieces from large railroads that were in existence for a long time aren't as valuable as items from smaller lines that only ran for a short spell.

RAZORS

Straight-edged razors with fancy handles of sterling, silver plate, stag, pearl, and ivory are the most desirable and the rarest. If the maker's name appears on the razor, it adds value.

RECORDS

The most desirable records are free of scratches and in their original jackets or boxes. Some collectors want only cylindrical records from the 1800s. Others seek 78 rpm records. It's only within the last few years that 33 rpm records have had any value as collectibles. Most collectors specialize in a certain type of music—jazz, rock, classical, ballads, or those performed by specific artists or groups.

ROSEVILLE

Baskets, planters, cookie jars, vases, and tea sets are among the most popular items made in Roseville, Ohio, from the 1880s to the 1950s. Later pieces were produced in great numbers, so they don't command the high prices of those made earlier. Unfortunately, some of most valuable pieces were produced during a period when the factory used only paper labels, many of which have been lost over the years. This category of collectible should be studied before you invest much money in it.

SALT AND PEPPER SHAKERS

Figural salt and pepper shakers can be purchased inexpensively at most garage sales. A very strong collectible, shakers fall into several categories and most serious collectors concentrate on just one or two of them. Categories include: Blacks, turn-arounds, nodders, miniatures, souvenirs, wooden shakers, advertising, airlines, metal shakers, etc. They may be in the form of animals, fruits and vegetables, household objects, buildings, etc.

SCOUTING MEMORABILIA

Boy Scout items are more popular than Girl Scout items, although the Girl Scouts are beginning to gain interest. Old handbooks, uniforms, hats, badges, pins, pocketknives, games, etc., are sought, usually by people who remember them from their childhoods. Condition is important and first edition handbooks bring much more than later editions.

SHAWNEE POTTERY

Planters, vases, and cookie jars are the most desirable pieces to collectors; dinnerware has a very small following. This company, open from 1937 until 1961 in Zanesville, Ohio, used many marks. Some have the word *Shawnee* in them; other marks were *USA #*___, and *Kenwood.*

SNOW BABIES

From the early 1900s to the 1930s, bisque dolls measuring one- to two-inches tall and dressed in white snow suits with a rough finish were produced mostly in Germany. Made in all types of poses from skiing, skating, and sleigh riding to dancing and singing, these cute figures were used on postcards and on some porcelain articles and made into confections. The figurines have been reproduced, but they lack the details of the originals.

SOUVENIR SPOONS

Teaspoons, coffee spoons, and orange spoons made of sterling silver or silver plate and depicting scenes from various places, from Niagara Falls to the World's Fairs, have been collected since the 1890s. Some spoons have enamel crests. Condition and material are very important. Sterling, of course, commands a higher price than silver plate. Avoid spoons with any damage as they're very hard to sell unless they're so rare that a collector will overlook flaws.

SPORT CARDS

Baseball card collectors spent almost one billion dollars to buy twelve billion cards in 1991. Baseball cards are the most sought of the sports cards, with football, basketball, and hockey following distantly and in that order of desirability. Mint condition is important. Topps, Fleer, Dunruss, Top Deck, and Bowman are the best known manufacturers. Approximately eighty-five percent of sports card collectors are male. So many of these cards have been reproduced in recent years that the forecast for these modern examples on the secondary market is dim.

STANGL BIRDS

These beautiful ceramic birds, fashioned after Audubon prints, were produced by the Stangl Potter of Trenton, New Jersey during the late 1930s and early 1940s. All are marked with *Stangl;* most examples have the initials of the artist in blue underglaze.

THIMBLES

Condition is important to the value of a thimble; they're judged as either mint, excellent, fair, or poor. Thimbles with advertising or political themes are popular. Post-1960s political thimbles are known as *brummagem,* which means showy but cheap. Many thimbles were made of gold or silver with intricate decorations on the tops. These are highly prized.

TOY SOLDIERS

Only excellent- to mint-condition soldiers are desirable to add to a collection, and since toy soldiers often suffered rough treatment in small hands, desirable condition is difficult to find. These playthings, made from 1930 to the 1950s, come in boxed sets, and the box is an important component of this collectible. Not only does a box complete the set, the design reveals when the set was made. Don't purchase any soldiers that appear to be repainted.

WATCH FOBS

Unless you've studied this collectible field and are knowledgeable in it, only buy fobs that have advertising or some other form of trademark on the back. Blank fobs are usually, but not always, reproductions. Of course, crocheted, hand-beaded, or other handcrafted one-of-a-kind fobs aren't marked.

WELLER WARE

From 1893 to 1948 Weller pottery was made in Zanesville, Ohio. All but the early pieces, including Lonhuda and Louwelsa, are fairly common. Weller figurals of animals are popular among collectors. Weller had several markings but all of them contained the word *Weller*.

WHISKEY BOTTLES

Commemorative bottles; bottles in the shapes of Texas, Rhode Island, or any other state; bottles depicting planes, trains, cowboys, Indians, animals, circus figures;

bottles with gambling motifs, political themes, or sporting subjects are all collectibles. James Beam Distilling Company, the major maker of these bottles, has offered whiskey in collectible bottles since 1953. Ezra Brooks, J. W. Dant, Hoffman, Old Fitzgerald, Old Mr. Boston, and McCormick are a few of the other collectible names.

WITCH BALLS

Handblown glass balls varying in size from three- to eight-inches were hung in windows to ward off witches during the 1700s. Made in many colors, these delightful balls have a small following of collectors.

CHAPTER 4

The Auction Psychology: To Beat 'em, Join 'em

As good merchandise becomes harder to find, more and more dealers turn away from auctions and look for inventory elsewhere. Admittedly, auction prices have soared in the last couple of years, but we still find this avenue for buying an invaluable one. There is always that "sleeper"—the treasure that's been overlooked or that the auctioneer has knocked down sooner than he or she should have. There are damaged items that, if you know how to fix them, can be sensational buys. There are rare, truly valuable articles that, because most dealers are unfamiliar with them, go for many times less than their worth.

We love this business—all aspects of it—but the part we love most is attending auctions. We love the excitement of discovering a piece of merchandise, realizing that it's a treasure, and hoping against hope that no one else at the auction knows its worth; the fun of looking over the items to be auctioned off and selecting those in which we're interested; the emotional highs and lows of bidding, sometimes winning other times losing the desired object. And finally, we especially love taking our purchases home and assessing whether we bought smart or made mistakes. It's all part of the auction mystique.

Auction Houses: How They Differ

PRESTIGIOUS AUCTION HOUSES

There are many different types of auctions. Sotheby's, Christie's, and several other large, prestigious houses are at the top of the ladder and handle the very best merchandise. It would seem then that these places are out of reach to all but the dealers who have lots of money to spend. This isn't always the case, however, because these top-of-the-line auction houses almost always have a few average pieces in every auction. By average we don't mean inferior. We're referring to items that might be the most desirable offerings at a middle-class auction house, but which are mundane to the sophisticated buyer at Sotheby's. In fact, these items may seem so mundane in comparison to the other unusual fare that's being auctioned that they have no appeal. When this is the case, an average dealer with an average pocketbook can purchase the items for far less than he or she would have to pay at a much less ritzy auction house. It's sort of like putting five-and-dime store merchandise in a leading Fifth Avenue department store—it's not what customers are accustomed to, and they won't buy it. These "biggie" auction houses also have secondary auctions offering less prestigious merchandise; these secondary auctions precede the main auction or take place simultaneously.

FINE AUCTION HOUSES

Descending the ladder a bit, fine auction houses carry a variety of merchandise but no junk. These are attended by retail customers and a wide mix of dealers but usually not by flea market dealers. Not only are these auctions fun to attend, but they're great places to learn about merchandise. You can see and touch quality things. Study backstamps. Experience, firsthand, the prices these items bring and compare them with similar items listed in price guides. Even if you can't buy at these auctions at first, it's a good idea to attend one every once in awhile.

COUNTRY AUCTIONS

Country auctions are held in barns, old houses, or outside during good weather (and sometimes when the weather isn't so good). On a sunny spring or summer day, it's delightful to sit and enjoy the fresh air while you bid on items for your inventory. At some auctions, food vendors sell snacks and sandwiches. You may prefer to pack a lunch or supper for yourself. At most of these auctions, you'll need to carry your own chair. We keep folding chairs in our van so that if we're out and see an auction we'd like to attend, we don't have to stand.

Many country auctions have great primitives for sale. Many feature old tools—fast sellers in some areas. Still others just have tired-looking furniture and household goods to offer and really qualify as junk auctions.

ESTATE AUCTIONS

Some auctions are held at the estate where the merchandise offered is housed. People put entire estates up for auction for a variety of reasons, but the most common one is that the owner has passed away, and those who've inherited the property want to dispose of it. Sometimes family members will go through the home, taking what they want for themselves before the contents are turned over to an auctioneer. When this happens, the good stuff is very often skimmed off and what's left is inferior. But if family members aren't knowledgeable about antiques, they may only take more modern pieces they think of as valuable. Other times and according to estate sale rules, no one in the family is allowed to take so much as a teaspoon. The theory here is that family members can bid on what they want, and the money from the sale will be divided evenly among the heirs.

Bidding against a family member can be tough. A daughter may remember when her mother rocked her to sleep in a fine old rocker and be willing to pay almost anything to have it. A son may have fond memories of his father's electric train collection. Or a granddaughter may want the old spool bed, remembering how the bedding was always turned down for her on the nights she visited. It's not easy to put a price on nostalgia. We try not to bid against family members. There are generally many valuable items left in which they have no interest.

REGIONAL AUCTION HOUSES

There are numerous small, regional auction houses that offer whatever merchandise they manage to get from consignors. Sometimes these auctions are wonderful, and sometimes they're a waste of time. You may attend an auction one week and find an assortment of treasures you'd love to own and go back to the same auction house with the same auctioneer the next week and be confronted with nothing but junk. Auctioneers have to find merchandise to sell. Auctioneers who have auctions on a regular basis—say, weekly—are more apt to have poor merchandise on occasion than auctioneers who wait until they have enough of the type of merchandise they like to handle before they hold an auction.

AUCTION HOUSES WITHOUT A "HOUSE"

Some auctioneers—usually, but not always, beginners or part-time auctioneers—conduct auction sales in rented facilities. Locations might include the lodge of a fraternal organization, a fire hall, a church basement, or a hotel. These auctions are usually very informal. And if the auctioneer is a part-timer, he or she may not be as well informed about the merchandise as someone who makes a full-time career of running auction sales. Thus, some good items may slip through at bargain prices. The only trouble with these auctions is that you usually have to remove your purchases the night of the sale because the hall has been rented only for that evening. This can pose a problem if you buy a large piece of furniture and need to make arrangements to have it transported to your house or shop.

Auction Strategies: The Nitty Gritty

PREVIEWING MERCHANDISE

The better auctions have a preview a day or two before the sale. This presale exhibit may even run for two or three days. Other auctions have preview hours just prior to the sale. It's a sound practice to attend a preview for at least an hour. Take that time to thoroughly examine all of the merchandise to be sold and write down the names of any articles that interest you. Some auction houses do not allow you to handle the merchandise without asking to see a specific piece. We find this acceptable only at very fine auctions that exhibit expensive, delicate, or small items. Middle-class auction houses using this practice are, in our opinion, trying to intimidate their clientele. Few people will ask to examine more than a few items. Therefore, most people will end up bidding blind on merchandise that may be damaged or just may not be what they perceived it to be when viewing it from a distance. We avoid auctions where we can't handle and examine what's to be offered.

The larger auction houses, and some of the smaller but nicer ones, have catalogs listing all merchandise to be sold at an auction. These items appear by number in the catalog in the order in which they'll be offered at the auction. Some catalogs are printed in full color and are sent to potential bidders around the world. If these potential bidders, say in Europe, are interested in a piece, they may plan to bid by phone or submit a written bid to be executed at the auction. Many of the more detailed catalogs include a

Previewing Merchandise

pre-auction price estimate of each piece to be auctioned. This is the amount that the auctioneer and/or staff anticipate the piece will bring at the actual auction. This is, however, only their estimate and is sometimes way off. If there is no listed pre-auction estimate, talk to the auctioneer, who will often give you an opinion of what an item will bring. Be advised that while these colorful listings are elegant to look at, the merchandise offered in them is far beyond the reach of the average dealer. However, many smaller auction houses print lists with a number and description of each piece. Most catalogs, whether they're plain or fancy, are for sale to auction goers. A few auctioneers give them away. We find these listings invaluable.

When we attend a preview we use the list as a guide. As we carefully examine each item of merchandise, we make a star beside those in which we're very interested, a plus beside those we might want at the right price, and a minus beside those we don't want at any price. We note any damage to an article.

Merchandise is sold in lots. A lot may consist of only one item or may be comprised of two, three, or many articles. A lot can be the entire contents of a tray or box. If an auction is cataloged, the merchandise will have two numbers on it (unless it all comes from the same place or the same consignor). One of these numbers is the lot number and will coincide with the number in the catalog. The other number is the consignor's number and of little interest to the auction goer.

When you attend a presale, try to see everything. Look

carefully even at a piece that doesn't really appeal to you. If you don't and that piece goes inexpensively at the auction, you may be tempted to bid on it even though you haven't examined it. Or, conversely, you may be afraid to bid on it because you didn't look closely enough. We find that when we take a chance on something we haven't seen, it almost always turns out to be a disaster, and we end up saying, "Oh, that's why it went so cheap!"

Write down a description of those items you'd like to own. If you don't know what they're worth, try looking them up in a price guide. It's a good idea to carry one with you to auctions. Many dealers view this as the mark of a rank amateur. So what! We've seen these very dealers who look down their noses at price guides, bid many times what an item lists for in a guide. And we've seen these same items sit in their booths year after year. Your price guides are only guides. But consulting them can keep you from making costly mistakes. Later, during the auction, you can write down on your catalog the price that each lot brings. In this way, you'll create your own price guide.

During the preview, write down how much you're willing to pay for an item you want beside its catalog listing. We have found that most auction goers think in round numbers. In other words, they're willing to pay $10, $15, $100, or $150 for an item. We select the next highest amount for our maximum bids. For instance, for a vase that we can sell for $20 and would like to buy for $10, we are willing to bid up to $12.50 if necessary. A dry sink for which we'd ask $300, we'll pay $160. This bidding psychology has paid off for us. Although we don't always double our money, we do make a profit. We often have the high bid precisely because we don't think in round numbers.

Since auctioneers have to have merchandise in order to hold their auctions, and merchandise isn't always easy to get, some auctioneers resort to a practice known as "salting." This simply means that they include in an auction merchandise that really doesn't belong. For instance, suppose an auctioneer has an estate to sell, but the estate doesn't include enough merchandise to have an auction that will last very long. The choice may be to bring in merchandise from another estate or another source and sell it as if it came from the original estate. Or, in another example, the auctioneer may schedule an auction at his or her auction house and find that merchandise is in short supply. The answer may be to "salt" the auction with brand new items, such as new carnival glass, depression glass, or art deco pieces. We don't see anything wrong with this practice as long as the auctioneer presents the material as what it is. If the auctioneer holds up a *new* bowl and says something like, "I have here a lovely amethyst carnival bowl in the thistle pattern," we take exception. But if the explanation continues, "It's newer, but it's nice," the auctioneer is not claiming the bowl to be anything that it's not. Many people are eager to own a bowl like this whether it's new or old. But they should be aware of the difference because that difference dictates the value.

PRE-AUCTION PREPARATIONS AND OTHER POINTERS

When you attend an auction, you should carry a tape measure so you'll know if the blanket chest you like will fit into the space you planned, or if the lamps are really too tall for your booth, or if the picture frame is large enough. You also need a magnifying glass. The manufacturer's marks on some pieces are very difficult to discern with the naked eye. You want to carry a magnet so that you won't be fooled into thinking a brass-coated statue, headboard, or inkwell is solid brass. (Solid brass doesn't take a magnet.) You need a pen and a pad of paper on which to write down what you're interested in bidding on if there's no catalog and on which to keep track of your purchases.

You'll need wrappers to protect your acquisitions and boxes in which to transport them. Many auction houses have paper for their customers and a supply of boxes. But others don't provide these items, and those that do frequently run out before the evening ends. Supplying these items is, after all, a courtesy not an obligation. We prefer to carry our own wrappers and boxes. We don't like newspaper because it offers scant protection and is so messy. We use moisture-proof bed and chair pads, which can often be found in supermarkets next to baby diapers. (These are discussed further in Chapter 7.) They can be used again and again. We add a few new ones and discard the most worn about once every two years. And because they have handles, banana boxes are our choice for packing. They're so much easier to carry.

You may want to carry a chair pad with you. Most auction seats are hard. One of the pads made for kitchen chairs is ideal; the pads are available at most department stores.

HOW TO REGISTER AND WHAT TO DO THEN

How to Register

When you arrive at an auction, you need to register with a clerk or member of the auction house. There is no charge to do this. You'll receive a paddle or a sign with a number on it. This is your bidding number, and any purchases you make will be assigned to it. If you attend an auction house on a regular basis for any length of time, you may be assigned your own number. Every time you go to that auction house, you'll be given it to use.

The first time you register with an auctioneer, you need to show the clerk your tax number (if one is required in your state). That means that you won't have to pay tax on any of your purchases. Successful bidders without tax numbers must add whatever the sales tax is in the state in which the auction is held to the amount they spend.

Arrive early enough to get seated in the area of the auction house you like best. We prefer the front row. Other dealers like the back row. Everyone has preferences and reasons for them. We find that we can see the merchandise better, and hear what's being said about it by the auctioneer and the runners much better, if we're in the front.

One night we arrived at an auction late and had to settle for a seat in the middle of the house. We didn't even have time to properly inspect the merchandise before the auction began. An oil painting came up and Joan bid on it, getting it for a low price. The next item was an oil on a tin. It looked good from the middle of the house. It also must have looked good to a man in the back of the house because he bid Joan up to a fairly high price. When we collected our items we saw, to our horror, that the tin was so badly pitted that the picture was absolutely worthless. We'd broken two of our rules on this one. Joan bid on merchandise we hadn't inspected, and she continued bidding on the assumption that the man in the back knew the value of the piece or he wouldn't have bid on it. You can never bid on what you assume is the opposition bidder's knowledge.

RULES OF THE HOUSE, SPOKEN AND UNSPOKEN

In most auction houses, you're asked not to remove anything you buy from the premises until you pay for it. We've found that once we become regular customers, the auction house will disregard that rule and allow us to carry merchandise to our van. This is much easier than trying to hold onto a full set of dishes, a pair of lamps, or a picture. However, if the auction house at which you're buying won't let you remove a mounting pile of purchases until you pay, the staff will generally find a spot in the building to hold them for you.

We aren't entirely comfortable with this practice. First, people coming late to the auction or those who simply weren't paying attention often think that this merchandise, which has been set aside, is merchandise that has not come up for bid yet. They handle it, examine it, and on occasion accidentally damage it. When this happens, the auction house bears none of the responsibility. You have, in effect, purchased the items and must pay for them. There are times when the individual who did the damage will offer to pay for the goods, times when they will refuse to do so, and times when you won't even know how your merchandise was damaged. Second, you have to keep an eye on the spot chosen to stash your items, and this takes your attention away from the auction and what the auctioneer is saying. Failure to watch your purchases makes them an inviting find for any light-fingered person in attendance. We always prefer to take possession of our purchases immediately after we've won the bid.

Most, but certainly not all, auctioneers are fairly honest. But remember they're not working for you and me as buyers, they're working for the seller. It's the seller who pays the commission, except when there's a buyer's fee. This fee, which usually amounts to ten percent of the purchase price of an item, is paid by the person who buys the item with the highest bid. The practice of charging a buyer's fee is gaining favor among auctioneers, and auction goers are not pleased. If an auctioneer is charging a ten percent buyer's fee, he or she can afford to offer to sell an estate for only a ten percent seller's fee instead of the usual twenty percent fee. This is an attractive offer for the seller. A few of the really high-priced auction houses are flirting with the idea of raising their buyer's fees to fifteen percent.

A good auctioneer will make every item seem as desirable as possible. He may hold glass pieces against black velvet to show them off to their best advantage. He may display the good side of a quilt, neglecting to point out that the reverse side is in tatters. He may not tell you that the carnival glass bowl he's holding is a reproduction, hot off the assembly line, and not an old example. He may do all these things and still be a good auctioneer. One of the best auctioneers we know will hold up an item and with great enthusiasm say something like, "Ladies and gentlemen, look here. This is a genuine Putterstown Pottery dish." Of course, no one has ever heard of Putterstown Pottery, but he is so excited about the piece that the uninitiated are certain it must be of great value. The bidding starts. If it doesn't go along well, he may admonish, "Come on folks. This is a great piece of Putterstown Potter." This usually stimulates more action and the piece is knocked down for much more than it's worth. Has the auctioneer been dishonest? We don't think so. He's done what the seller has asked him to do—gotten the best price possible. And he hasn't lied. The merchandise is a piece of Putterstown Pottery. A good auctioneer, like a good stand-up comic, knows how to work the room.

TERMS OF THE SALE

Just prior to the beginning of an auction, the auctioneer will probably announce the terms and conditions of the sale, telling auction goers how to pay for their purchases. Some auction houses will accept only cash. Most will also allow you to pay by check if they know you. If you don't live in the state in which the auction is taking place, you may find that your out-of-state check isn't acceptable. Some auction houses are set up to accept credit cards, although they often add a small charge for doing so.

It's at this point that the auctioneer will also let you know whether or not this is an absolute auction (where everything will be sold no matter how low the highest bid is) or if some of the items have reserves on them. As a rule, auctioneers prefer to handle merchandise with no reserves. But if an auctioneer is offered a desirable estate or assortment of merchandise and the consignor won't part with some of the pieces under a certain price, the auctioneer will go along with the consignor's wishes rather than have the merchandise go to another auctioneer. In this announcement, you will also be told whether there are any left bids and who will execute them for the bidder.

Listen carefully to what the auctioneer has to say. You may be asked to remove all merchandise from the premises at the end of the auction. Or you may be told that large items can be left a day or two while you make arrangements to have them transported. You may find that the auction house will deliver them for you. Of course, you'll have to pay them a fee. If you're a regular customer who spends a lot of money with this auction house over the course of a year, they may deliver without charging you.

BIDDING STRATEGIES AND OTHER CONSIDERATIONS

You can get the best buys at auctions at the very beginning when the crowd is usually thin and hasn't warmed up yet. People tend to save their money for the special items they've selected. The end of an auction is also prime time for bargains. Many bidders have departed with their newfound treasures, and those who remain have often spent or at least made great inroads into the amount they have to spend. Of course, auctioneers aren't stupid and they don't bring up the best merchandise during these times. We still find that we can make a substantial profit on most items we buy at the beginning and end of an auction. This isn't our best merchandise, to be sure, but it includes the lower-priced items that are bread and butter for most dealers.

Another time for good buys is when two or more auctions are scheduled for the same time. Obviously, no dealer can be in two places at once. If you travel in pairs, as we do, you can split up, each one attending a different auction.

Bidding has almost become an art form. Everyone has his or her own way of signaling the auctioneer. A wink, a nod, the wiggle of a finger, the wave of a hand—it's a wonder auctioneers can follow all these personalized methods. We bid by holding up our card. It's easier. We know we'll be seen, and auctioneers vastly prefer it. Since we already know how high we're willing to go for any given item, someone trying to bid us up is going to get stuck—not us. We do make our mistakes, but for the most part, we don't go any higher than the amount we previously wrote down as the top we would pay for an item. This isn't always easy. Auctions are exciting; it's tempting to go that one more bid, and then just one more. If you give in to this temptation, you may find yourself holding your breath and hoping someone will top your bid and get you off the hook.

Some veteran auction goers like to get in the bidding early. Others feel they're better off invoking the element of surprise and only start their bidding when it appears that another bidder has won the prize. And this does work sometimes. A person who thinks the bidding has stopped and that his or her bid is highest may be shocked into silence, thus losing the item in question. We prefer to get in at the beginning of the action, although we usually wait until the auctioneer has dropped the opening or asking bid. For instance, the auctioneer says, "How about $50 for this Shawnee cookie jar . . . $25 . . . $10 . . . who'll give me $10?" If someone jumps in at $10, we're quick to pick up the bid at $12.50. When to bid is personal, and we suggest joining in when you feel the time is right for you to do so.

Leaving a bid can be risky! There are a few, but fortunately not many, auctioneers who customarily start the bidding with the full amount of a solitary left bid. If you leave a bid and get the merchandise for the full amount you authorized the auctioneer to bid on your behalf, you might have cause to be suspicious. If this happens several times with the same auctioneer, you'd be wise not to leave bids with him or her again.

While we're on the subject of dishonesty, a few auctioneers pull bids out of the air. This is most apt to happen if the auctioneer perceives a bidder as being inexperienced and unfamiliar with the merchandise. The auctioneer may hold up an item of little value and after finally getting a bid, look to another spot well behind or to the side of the bidder and act as though someone had raised the bid. This may happen several times before the article is knocked down to the first—and actually only—bidder. We saw a shocking example of this at an auction where a woman bid on a very inferior cabinet. She bid up to $700 for a piece not worth $100 before another member of the audience saw what the auctioneer was doing and called him on it. Of course, the auctioneer denied culpability, saying he "thought someone else was bidding." But the woman got off the hook and ended up buying the cabinet for $75. Auctioneers who pull this sort of thing usually have short careers.

Auctioneers have a way of talking that imparts, to those who listen carefully, valuable information about the merchandise being auctioned. The auctioneer may say, "This *looks* like sterling to us." That invariably means the piece is unmarked and hasn't been tested. It may, indeed, be sterling. On the other hand, it may not be. If you buy it, test it, and find that it isn't sterling, don't go back to the auctioneer to complain. The statement was, "This looks like sterling to us." There were no guarantees. Or you may hear, "We think this is a brass horn from an Italian gondola, but buy it for what you perceive it to be." The auctioneer is clearly stating that the auction house takes no responsibility for the authenticity of the item.

What if you purchase a piece of glass only to find when the runner delivers it to you that there's a chip in it, rendering it almost useless to you? The better auctioneers will allow you to return any glass or china items that aren't perfect *unless,* and this is an important unless, they've said the piece was sold "as is." You're expected to inspect whatever you're interested in before an auction or at least before you bid on it. But auctioneers realize that you may look at a cut-glass vase one-half hour before the auction starts, examine it thoroughly, and find it in perfect condition; then another person may pick up that vase, knock it against something else and chip it. However, other items, such as furniture, mirrors, pictures, lamps, etc., which aren't as readily damaged, are usually not accepted back by an auctioneer. If you find you've bought a broken piece of glass or porcelain, quietly show it to one of the runners who can usually take care of it for you.

Although condition is very important, there are certain times when you may purchase damaged goods. Soft paste items that have weathered time and handling are usually chipped a bit. While perfect examples are preferable, this chipping doesn't make a piece unsalable. There just aren't enough perfect examples of soft paste to go around, so collectors will settle for less. Damaged merchandise that you can repair may be a real buy. (See Chapter 5 on repairs.) But it's best to practice on a worthless piece first, saving the quality articles until you've perfected whatever type of specialized repair they need.

Logistics of Check Out

Write down everything you buy and the price you bid for each piece. When you check out, be sure that your total tallies with that of the cashier. If you're at a house where there's a buyer's premium, you'll pay an additional amount (usually ten percent) above the purchase price. If your total and the cashier's total differ, go over each item to see if you're being charged more than you bid. Look to see if something you haven't purchased has been charged inadvertently to your number. Most cashiers are pleasant about doing this. If you have a tax number make sure you're not being charged tax.

Logistics of Check Out

When you check out, the cashier should give you a list of your purchases. Today most are computer lists, but some auction houses do everything by hand. You may be handed a stack of small cards. Each one will have the description of a lot you purchased on it, what you paid, what your bidder's number was, and the date. As we enter our purchases into our inventory book, we check off the items on the list of cards.

Taking auction treasures home; unpacking them; assessing them; deciding whether it's been a good auction or one at which you made mistakes; sometimes finding that you've picked up something that's worth far more than you'd thought when you bid on it, is almost as much fun as the auction itself.

A Glossary of Terms

ABSENTEE BID

A bid that has been left with the auctioneer or a member of the auction house by a person who is unable to attend the auction but is interested in purchasing merchandise that will be sold. Unless there are two absentee bids, an auctioneer must start the bidding from the floor and only raise it in reasonable increments from the absentee bid. If there are two or more absentee bids on the same item, an auctioneer starts the bidding with the second highest absentee bid.

ABSOLUTE AUCTION

An auction at which everything will be sold to the highest bidder. There is no minimum amount of money under which an item will not be sold.

AS IS

A term applied by the auctioneer to a piece of merchandise that is damaged.

AS IT IS AND WHERE IT IS

Often said by auctioneers to warn bidders that the merchandise is sold to the highest bidder in whatever condition it's in and on the spot where it sits. The seller is not responsible for any damage or for moving the item.

ATTRIBUTION

Knowing who made, wrote, or painted an article, book, or picture, etc. If, for instance, a print is signed by Maxfield

Parrish, it is worth far more than a print of similar quality signed by an unknown artist. The names Frank Lloyd Wright, R. Lalique, or Jose Clemente Orozco give value to merchandise that might otherwise be overlooked.

BUY ON YOUR OWN KNOWLEDGE

A phrase often used by an auctioneer to tell bidders that regardless of what the auctioneer says he *thinks* a piece of merchandise is, he isn't responsible if it turns out to be something else.

BUYER'S PREMIUM

The amount, usually ten percent, of the auction sales price that an auctioneer charges the winning bidder over and above the amount for which the item was sold. This is not done at all auctions, but it is a growing trend.

CONSIGNMENT

Giving an auctioneer (or a dealer) merchandise to sell for which they will receive a percentage (usually twenty percent) of the selling price.

CONSIGNOR

The person whose goods are being auctioned.

HAMMER PRICE

The highest amount that has been bid when the auctioneer says, "sold" or pounds his hammer. Anyone trying to bid after this point will not be recognized, even though the auctioneer would get more for the article in question.

JUNK AUCTION

An auction of household goods and other miscellaneous items rather than a sale of antiques and collectibles.

KNOCKED DOWN

An auction term meaning sold. Often used in referring to the price. For instance, "The desk was knocked down for $250."

LEFT BID

Same as Absentee Bid.

LOT NUMBER

A number given to and posted on all merchandise that comes from the same consignor. Any one auction may have goods from a number of consignors. The lot number is used so that whoever is recording the sales will credit the right consignor with the sale of his or her merchandise.

ON THE BLOCK

The item that is being auctioned at any given time is said to be "on the block."

PRESALE ESTIMATE

The amount that an auctioneer or a member of his staff estimates that any given object will bring at auction.

PRESALE EXHIBIT

The time, prior to an auction, when merchandise may

be viewed and assessed by potential buyers. This is sometimes the day of the auction and sometimes a day or two before the sale.

PREVIEW

Same as Presale Exhibit.

RESERVE

A price below which an item will not be sold. If it fails to get a high enough bid, the article in question will be withdrawn from the auction.

RUNNERS

The people who hold up the merchandise that's being auctioned and deliver it to the highest bidder.

SMALLS

A term used in referring to any small, easily transported item that's being auctioned.

TELEPHONE BID

A bid executed over the phone by an absent bidder. A member of the auction house staff tells the phone bidder what's being bid at the auction house. The phone bidder in turn gives a counterbid. This continues until the item in question is knocked down to the highest bidder.

UNRESERVED

Items that will be sold at auction to the highest bidder no matter how low that bid may be.

CHAPTER 5

Housekeeping Hints: Clean and Repair Your Wares

The world of antiques and collectibles is not a perfect one. Most of the items you buy for resale will require cleaning; many will need repairing. Ideally, the merchandise you purchase should be in tip-top condition. In reality, you'll find nicks, scratches, and dents on some treasures that you thought were in perfect condition. Or you may buy a tray or box lot (several items sold for one price) at auction because you want one item and then find that you can make some of the other merchandise salable with a little patching. You may even damage something yourself either in transit or at your outlet. Then there's always the furniture that needs refinishing and/or regluing. There are clocks that won't run, and pieces of beautiful cut glass that are a little cloudy.

Whatever the reason, you're bound to have some soiled or damaged things on your hands. In this chapter we will pass on tips and procedures for cleaning and repairing that we have gleaned from our experience. They are intended for the novice with minor handyman/woman skills and common tools and products.

We firmly believe that to conceal a repair from a customer is bad business as well as unethical. And it has been our experience that few people will reject an item simply because they have learned it has been suitably repaired.

IMPORTANT PRECAUTIONS

•When working with any commercial chemical mixture such as glues, paints, varnishes, strippers, bleaches, cleaners, and polishes, be sure to read and follow the directions and warnings that accompany each product.

•When using unfamiliar chemicals that lack specific precautions, assume they are dangerous to breathe and handle and that they may harm exposed parts of your body.

•Work outdoors or in a well-ventilated room.

•Wear rubber gloves and keep your arms covered.

•Be careful of your face and eyes—protective goggles or glasses may be in order.

•Avoid splashing the chemicals, and when diluting or mixing harsh chemicals, add the stronger product into the weaker one.

•Glass containers, which are nonporous, are the best choice for handling chemicals.

•Dispose of your used chemicals responsibly. Call your local department of sanitation to find out how to dispose of toxic products correctly. Pouring certain household chemicals down drains can damage pipes and septic systems.

Cleaning and Polishing

BONE AND IVORY

Remove dirt and dust from bone and ivory objects with methylated spirit applied with a damp cloth, or use a soft-bristled brush for carved pieces. If the item is in good condition and without breaks or cracks, you can use a mild detergent and lukewarm water. Thoroughly dry immediately to avoid warping or cracking. For stubborn dirt, rub the area with methylated spirit and whiting. Dab a cotton wool pad, moistened with the methylated spirit, into the whiting and scrub as you would with a cleanser. Wipe off the residue using a clean cloth soaked with methylated spirit. End the cleaning process by polishing with a soft flannel cloth.

BRASS (See: Copper, Brass, and Bronze)

BRONZE (See: Copper, Brass, and Bronze)

CHINA AND POTTERY

Unless you definitely know that a piece of china or pottery is automatic dishwasher safe, clean by washing in lukewarm water and a mild detergent. The heat and water force of an automatic dishwasher can crack the surface, loosen the glue of any repairs, and damage transfer patterns and hand-painted designs. You can usually soak off grease and other stubborn dirt. If the design is underglaze, you may spot-clean the piece with a liquid household cleaner (the operative word here is *may*—test the cleaner on an obscure area of the object first). Wash the cleaner off immediately. Trade publications advertise products into which china can be dipped to give it a sparkling new look. We do not recommend these products because they are temporary and easily rinse off.

CLOCKS

Clock cases are made of a variety of materials—metal, wood, glass, plastic, etc.—so use whatever method is appropriate to clean those materials.

The most common cause of clock failure is dirt. Like everything else exposed to the earth's atmosphere, dust builds up inside clock cases. In modern clocks the works are usually in a dirt-free enclosure within the case, but the works of older clocks or their replicas have no such protection. Dust, soot, smoke, and other air-borne particles get into the case through loose-fitting backs, finger holes (for removing the backs), cracks, and open backs. Over the years this accumulated dirt, combined with moisture, creates a gummy substance that binds the moving parts. This process occurs sooner if the clock is not in use. In other words, to some degree, a working clock is self-cleaning. When the parts are in motion, they reduce the amount of dirt that settles on their surfaces. So the works of a clock that has been in storage are more likely to be frozen from grime than one that has been in use up to the time you bought it. However, clocks purchased at auctions, flea markets, etc., will have been idle for days or even years. For this reason, many clocks that appear in these markets are not in working order. However, many only need cleaning to restore their usefulness.

How do you know if a clock only needs cleaning to restore it to working order? There's no sure way for the amateur to know, but if the clock runs for a short time when you first wind it or shake it, the probability is high that dirt is the culprit.

There are three steps you can take to clean a clock. If the clock begins running in one of the first two stages, don't go on to the next.

First step: open the back to expose the works. If you have a mini-vac (a small vacuum cleaner for cleaning cameras, keyboards and electronic equipment), vacuum everything in sight—the top, bottom, and sides of the interior, and all the exposed areas of the works, including wheels, springs, pendulum anchor, etc. If you don't have a mini-vac, blow the interior out with a hand-held hair dryer, set on *no heat* and *low speed.* (Heat can expand the parts and cause them to bind.) If your hair dryer lacks a no heat setting, use a small, quality artist's brush to clean out the dirt. After you have brushed out all the dirt you can, blow off all the working parts with an empty atomizer. *Important: do not oil any of the parts!* Try to start the clock. Be sure it is level. If there is no response or the clock quits, try again. If you still don't have any success, move on to the second level of cleaning.

Second step: obtain an aerosol spray cleaner for audio, video, and computer drives. We bought the can we have on hand from a franchised electronic store. This product is a whiz for cleaning clock works. Just spray the works liberally—use the spray like you would a garden hose to clean off a walk or driveway. Don't worry about getting too much of the solvent in the clock, it quickly evaporates without a trace. OK, now start up the clock. Again, give it several tries. If nothing happens, consider moving on to the third step.

Third step: this method of cleaning is for the very brave or a professional. It is not likely you will want to go to this extreme for a few dollars profit. On the other hand, you should find it very educational and entertaining, or at least provocative. If you haven't disassembled a clock before it would be a good idea to take a book on basic clock repairing out of the library for reference. The instructions are simple: disassemble the works and clean them with solvent, dry, and wipe on a very light coat of clock oil. *Important: do not allow any oil on the teeth of gears!* Reassemble.

COPPER, BRASS, AND BRONZE

Copper and its two alloy metal derivatives, brass and bronze, tarnish quickly. For that reason, they are often treated with a coat of clear lacquer. Not only does the lacquer prevent a beautiful patina from developing on these metals, its removal is the bane of those of us who clean them. If the item is lacquered and the finish is uniform in color, our advice is to wipe it off with a damp cloth and leave it alone. *Do not wash lacquered metals in hot water—it cracks the finish.* On the other hand, if the lacquer is worn or scratched and spots of tarnish or discoloring have occurred, you will probably want to strip the lacquer and polish the metal. This may take some time, and you should determine if the piece can be priced to accommodate the additional labor.

Your local hardware store stocks lacquer removing products. They may or may not do the job. The trouble is that all lacquers are not equal, and one lacquer remover is not likely to remove all the different kinds of lacquer. So you pay your money and take your chances. We have had some luck in using non-oily fingernail polish remover (acetone is the main ingredient). But it doesn't always work either. Unfortunately, what always works is elbow grease, and that means work, hard work. Depending on the piece, it can take up to several hours of rubbing.

With grade fine, #0 steel wool, rub off the lacquer. These metals are easily scratched so, on flat surfaces, move the steel wool pad in one direction only. On round objects, like candlesticks, cup the pad in your hand and twist it around the piece in a corkscrew fashion. You will create tiny woodgrain-like scratches and you do not want them to crisscross. The pads will load up with lacquer and must be turned over and replaced frequently. When you have removed all the lacquer, buff the object in the same way with super-fine, #0000 steel wool. All the coarse marks should be replaced with finer ones from the #0000 pads. Rinse off all the steel wool dust and dry. Lastly, polish out the remaining scratches with jeweler's rouge or whiting. Rub in the same direction as you did with the steel wool pads until the piece is mirror smooth.

Cleaning and Polishing

Tarnished copper pieces that are free of lacquer can be cleaned with a paste of whiting and methylated spirits. The old-fashioned method of dipping half a lemon in salt and rubbing the object with it still works. A variation of that formula that has worked for us is to substitute a small rag soaked in lemon concentrate for the half lemon, sprinkle on salt, and rub away. Yet another recipe is to mix equal parts of salt and flour, add enough white vinegar to form a paste, and polish with a cloth.

Water spots can be removed with a paste of whiting and spirits of turpentine. After using any of the cleaning methods described here, rinse the object with clear water and polish dry.

While copper items are shaped from sheets of metal, brass (a mixture of copper and zinc) and bronze (a mixture of copper and tin) are usually cast. Both of these alloys are harder and stronger than copper, with bronze being the stronger metal. In the world of antiques, brass is more prevalent than either copper or bronze.

Brass that has caked-on dirt or grease can be cleaned with a 50% solution of household ammonia. If moderate corrosion is present, remove it with steel wool (using the same technique used to remove lacquer, as described above). If the corrosion is severe, rub it off with an emery cloth or medium-grade sandpaper, then follow with #0 and #0000 steel wool. Finish by polishing with jeweler's rouge.

To remove tarnish from brass, wipe with a solution of one tablespoon of salt, one tablespoon of white vinegar, and one pint of water. Rinse in clear water, dry, and buff with a soft cloth. For a really bright finish, buff with jeweler's rouge.

To restore the patina lost through cleaning, soak the brass object in boiling tea. Use one or two tea bags per quart of water. The longer the brass is bathed in tannic acid, the darker it gets, so check the object for color every five or ten minutes. We have used this method to harmonize new replacement brass hardware with the old.

There are two schools of thought regarding how to polish old brass. One way is to do whatever is necessary to obtain a sparkling, golden finish. The other is to refrain from polishing in order to retain the existing patina, thereby showing the quiet glow of age.

Bronze easily corrodes to green when it is not treated with lacquer. For outdoor objects such as sundials and garden statuary this is desirable—so much so that imitation corroded bronze finishes are used on these items. And it's not just the corrosion that is imitation. From the late nineteenth century through the 1930s, many of the "bronze" art nouveau and art deco figures and accessories were fake bronze because bronze castings were expensive to manufacture. White metal, pot metal, and spelter (cast zinc) were substituted with bronze-looking finishes.

If the object you have is really bronze and lightly corroded, you may rub off the corrosion with a coarse cloth. Heavier corrosion requires scraping with a brass brush. You can purchase these special brushes at a hardware store, or use the small brass brushes sold to clean suede leather. A 10% solution of white vinegar should remove any residue. Polish with a soft cloth to create a uniform patina.

GLASS

Most glassware will clean up with a simple hand bath in water and dishwashing detergent. Unless the glass is recent and undecorated and you know it is safe in an automatic dishwasher, clean it by hand. The water pressure and high temperature of an automatic dishwasher can crack older glass and loosen or wear away any applied design.

Stubborn stains and dirt will usually soak free overnight. If soil remains, rub the spots with liquid detergent applied with a nonabrasive scrub pad. Do not use abrasive fiber-type pads, steel wool, or abrasive cleaners—they will scratch the glass. If there is a design and it has been fired (baked) on, it will endure a light scrubbing with a plastic scrub pad. If the design was flashed on (not fired), it will not survive scrubbing. The design is probably fired on if the surface texture and sheen over the design is uniform with the rest of the glass. Thoroughly rinse off all detergent with water and dry the item with a soft cloth or paper towels.

Clouding, caused by minerals in the water, sometimes occurs on the inside of glass pitchers, decanters, and vases. You can remove clouding, if it isn't too heavy, by soaking the item in a 50% mixture of white vinegar and water. It may take several days of soaking.

Mirrors, glass in picture frames, glass-top tables, and other objects of sheet glass can all be cleaned with a mixture of two tablespoons of nonsudsy ammonia to one quart of water. White vinegar or alcohol can be substituted for ammonia, using the same proportions. Apply the solution with a spray bottle and wipe the object dry with half a sheet of newsprint. The printer's ink gives a special polish to glass. Of course, there are always commercial glass cleaners and paper towels.

If picture glass has dirt or fingerprints on the underside, you will need to take out the backing; if dirty, the print or matting should be cleaned at this time (see below for how to clean paper). The backs of mirrors can be cleaned gently with a cloth dampened in clear water—chemicals may damage the silvering. Reverse paintings on glass are very fragile and the underside should not be handled.

GOLD

Gold is virtually impervious to tarnish. If you have an article of gold that shows tarnish, it's probably gold-plated and the base metal is bleeding through to the surface. Items of gold, or gold and silver, can usually be cleaned easily by soaking in household ammonia overnight. If the item has been cemented, as with many pieces of jewelry, we advise just wiping the piece with an ammonia-soaked cloth or washing in a bath of dishwashing detergent and warm water. Rinse and polish with a soft cloth.

IVORY (SEE: BONE AND IVORY)

METAL (SEE: CHINA AND POTTERY)

OIL PAINTINGS

Older paintings take on a dark, dingy appearance. Surface dirt can be removed by wiping the picture with a cotton swab dipped in white spirit (from the hardware store). Do this with a light hand. Commercial oil painting cleaners are also available, along with instructions for their use. If the picture is still dingy, it calls for stronger measures. After an artist completes a painting, he or she protects it by applying a coat of varnish. In time this varnish becomes discolored. Over the years different varnishes have been used by artists, and there is no sure solvent that will take them all off. It's a matter of trying different products, and any one of them could ruin the painting. So if the painting is valuable, we recommend that you have it professionally stripped and revarnished.

PAPER

Lightly soiled book pages, prints, matting, and other kinds of paper goods with a nonglossy finish, can usually be cleaned up and made more marketable. Fingerprints and various smudges will often come off by rubbing them with white bread. If this fails, use a white art eraser. Easy does it. The idea is to lift the dirt without tearing the paper or damaging its fibers. Pencil marks and the like require a white art eraser. Rub as gently as possible, so as not to compress the fibers more than necessary.

For ink stains, foxing (brownish-yellow mildew stains), and other stains, dilute one-third laundry bleach to two-thirds water. Using an eyedropper or small brush, apply over the stained area. Let set ten minutes and blot with blotting paper or paper toweling. Brush clear water on and beyond the treated spot and blot with blotting paper or paper toweling several times until the bleach has been thoroughly removed. Repeat this rinsing process several times more to flush out all the bleach or the bleaching action will continue. Next, place the paper between two sheets of blotting paper on a flat surface and cover with a heavy, flat object, such as a book. After the paper has dried (in about twenty-four hours), carefully separate it from the blotting paper. If the stain is still present but lighter, repeat the full bleaching cycle. If the stain remains unaffected by the bleaching and the paper is a loose sheet, try immersing the sheet in a bath of a 2½ percent solution of Chloramine T.—a white bleaching powder obtainable from hardware stores. Soak for ten or twenty minutes and thoroughly rinse off. Dry between two sheets of blotting paper as described above. Repeat if necessary. This is a particularly good method for removing multiple stains and foxing where the stained area is large.

When using bleach it is best to err on the side of safety, initially using a weak solution for a short bath time. Also, the full effects of the bleach are only visible after the paper has dried, so wait until then to determine if the treatment needs to be repeated.

PEWTER AND BRITANNIA METAL

Pewter is an alloy of tin and a small quantity of lead, copper, antimony, or bismuth. It looks very much like lead and is comparatively soft and malleable. It was used extensively for household utensils until the mid-1800s; it is these items of pewter (also reproduction tankards) that are most often found in the trade.

If the piece is in good condition with a uniform patina,

polishing with a soft cloth should be sufficient. If there is corrosion, rub with a light abrasive powder, such as whiting or crocus powder, on an oily rag. Wipe clean with methylated spirits.

Britannia metal contains tin, antimony, and copper. Although it lacks any lead, it looks much like pewter when it is old. When new and highly polished, it looks like silver. In fact it was used as a poor man's silver until electroplating was invented, at which point it became a base metal for silver plate. Clean and polish as you would pewter.

POTTERY (SEE: CHINA AND POTTERY)

SILVER

Silver flatware and other items of sterling, European alloy of 80% silver and 20% copper, coin, or silver plate in good repair will only require the removal of tarnish followed by a polishing. Silver cleaners, called one-way products, are liquids that you either dip the silver pieces into, or spread over the surface of the silver and rinse off. They contain acid that is irritating to skin and has a strong pungent odor, but no rubbing is required—that comes when you polish.

Two-way products remove the tarnish and polish the silver. Three-way silver care products remove tarnish, polish, and chemically treat the silver to slow down the tarnishing process. These last two products come in paste form, contain a mild abrasive, and must be rubbed on—that is, you rub tarnish off with a cloth loaded with the paste. You then rinse off the paste and then buff the silver with a soft, dry cloth.

To make your own inexpensive silver polish, mix ammonia with whiting (ground chalk, sold at hardware stores) to form a paste. Polish the silver, rinse well, and buff dry. For a handy silver polishing cloth, mix one tablespoon of ammonia and one teaspoon of whiting in one cup of warm water. Soak an old napkin or piece of flannel in this mixture and allow to dry.

Silver items with a satin finish are best cleaned with a dip. The buffing or rubbing necessary to clean with a paste will produce an uneven shine on the finish and ruin the satin finish.

Silver with a dark, oxidized finish or design is difficult to clean. Both the dips and the abrasive pastes can damage it. However, the lesser of the two evils is the pastes. Use them as gingerly as possible. And rinse well.

Electrolysis is a fast, effortless, and inexpensive way to clean tarnish from silverware. We've successfully used it and found it particularly helpful with flatware that has a heavy design. All you need is baking soda and aluminum foil. We use a glass baking dish measuring about twelve inches by eight inches by two inches deep to hold the silver, but any convenient size will do. Cover the inside bottom of the dish with a sheet of aluminum foil and place the silver on it. Every piece must touch the aluminum. Next, bring one-and-a-half quarts of water to a boil, turn the heat off, and dissolve three-fourths of a teaspoon of baking soda in it. Pour this mixture over the silver so that every item is completely immersed, and allow to sit for a few minutes while the electrochemical process takes place. Remove the pieces as soon as they are free of tarnish and rinse off under warm water, dry, and then polish with a clean flannel cloth or a commercial silver cloth. Caution: this method may damage satin or oxidized finishes. And although we have never experienced a problem with electrochemical cleaning of hollow-handled knives and other cemented pieces, hot water can dissolve old or inferior glues.

Jeweler's rouge is a mild abrasive material that comes in bars and can be purchased at craft supply shops. It is used to polish various metals including silver and brass; it's also used to smooth scratches in glass. When buffing with a power wheel, hold the bar against the wheel in motion. This coats the wheel with rouge, a procedure that you must repeat during the polishing process. For manual polishing, just rub the rouge onto a soft cloth. Jeweler's rouge is very effective, but it collects in corners and crevices of designs during polishing and requires removal by further rubbing with clean cloths.

Silver items that have been exposed to salt become corroded in time if they are neglected. (Salt in the atmosphere causes silver chloride, or corrosion, to form.) This is a particular problem with silver salt shakers. If the piece is of high quality, take it to a professional to be cleaned. If the piece isn't worth the price of professional services, we offer two formulas that may salvage it.

For slightly corroded silver, mix a solution of 10% formic acid (obtained from a chemical supply house) to 90% water. Using a cotton swab, wipe the solution on the spot and rinse off immediately. For more stubborn cases, immerse the piece in a glass jar of the same solution for several hours and then thoroughly rinse off. *Caution: formic acid is caustic and must be handled with rubber gloves in a well-ventilated space.*

Badly corroded silver may also be cleaned with a 5% solution of citric acid (derived from citrus fruits) to 95% water. Apply this solution only to small areas at a time and quickly rinse off under running water. Repeat the process until all the corrosion has been treated.

GERMAN SILVER/NICKEL SILVER

German silver is the old name used for nickel silver. It is an alloy of nickel, copper, and zinc. Not a trace of silver is in it. It was introduced into England in the late 1700s, and because it looks like silver it was used as a cheap replacement. Like Britannia metal, nickel silver was also used as a base for silver-plated items. If *E.P. N. S.* is marked on the piece, it means it is electroplated nickel silver. Clean and polish as you would silver.

WOOD

Furniture and other objects made of wood, which have not been painted, will usually have a finish of lacquer, varnish, or acrylic. If not severely soiled, you can easily clean these finishes with a commercial cleaner polish. If grime is caked on, you can remove it with turpentine or paint thinner. These products will dissolve oil and grease along with the wax. Use a natural-bristled toothbrush to clean the crevices, dry, and polish.

Furniture that has been neglected and is in bad condition with little or no finish can be brush-scrubbed with soap and water. Rinse off with clear water, wipe as dry as possible, and liberally rub down with paint thinner. The paint thinner will eliminate, or at least reduce to a minimum, the grain swelling. Unless you intend to refinish the piece, rub down the surfaces with generous amounts of linseed oil or furniture oil.

Repairing

There's a considerable difference between repairing an antique or collectible and restoring it. To repair an object, as we understand the term, is to return it to a usable or working condition, and, if possible, improve its appearance. Restoration, on the other hand, means to restore the item to its original condition. Restoration requires professional knowledge, tools, and materials, and, therefore, is beyond the scope of this book. In this section on repairing objects, we describe techniques that we believe a dealer lacking special skills can follow.

When you consider repairing a dish, toy, chair, or whatever, keep your purpose in mind. If you are doing the project strictly for profit, then consider the time and materials you are about to invest. If you pay yourself minimum wage for two hours of labor to repair an item that will only bring you ten dollars, you're losing money. (If you want to charge yourself twenty-five dollars an hour for simple repairs, we suggest you look for a less expensive workman.) If you paid five dollars for the plate, your loss is even greater. On the other hand, if you paid five dollars for the plate because it was damaged, and with two hours of labor can sell it for sixty dollars, then repairs are worthwhile. And if you are in the business for fun as well as profit, you can write off the labor to entertainment and/or education.

BONE AND IVORY

Most bone and ivory objects are best left alone, but if a piece is badly damaged, paraffin can be used to improve its appearance and protect it. For cracks, prewarm the piece with a hair blow dryer or in a warm kitchen, or the like. You want it warm, not hot. Melt a crayon (colored paraffin) of the right color and pour into the crevice or apply with a brush. If the bone or ivory is so brittle or fragile that it may break apart, it can be sheathed in a thin coat of wax. Heat paraffin (sold at grocery stores for canning) until it has liquidized, turn off the heat, and dunk the (prewarmed) piece. Dip half the object, let it cool, then dip the other half. Hold the piece over the pot and let the excess paraffin run off. Whatever excess wax is on the bottom can be trimmed off when it has cooled. Buff, and the piece will be more secure against the hazards of handling.

CHINA AND POTTERY

Having chipped, cracked, and broken china and pottery pieces in your inventory is an inevitability in this business. However carefully you make your purchases, or transport your goods, or watch over them on display, damaged goods appear. When it occurs, you can send them to auction, try to sell them as is, or increase their salability by repairing them. Practice makes perfect—or at least improves the results. So expect less than perfection with your first attempts. The more experience you have in repairing, the better the results.

China repair kits are available and include special products that can do a remarkable job. (You will find them for sale in trade publications.) However, practice is still required for success.

Pieces such as handles that have broken off or plates that have been dropped can be glued back in place. Use one of the glues that specifically states it is for china repair. You'll find an assortment at hardware and dime stores. The pieces should be clean and should fit tightly together. Make provisions ahead of time to support the pieces while the glue hardens. Depending on the piece, it may require only a flat surface, or it may call for a sculptured support. In the case of the latter, a gluing box may be the answer. To make one, just cut down a cardboard box that is larger than the object you intend to glue. Its height should accommodate about five inches of filler plus the depth of the object to be glued. For filler, use clean, dry sand (purchased at an aquarium supply store), or rice. Take the object to be glued or, better yet, a similar piece—say, a matching saucer—and mold a resting place in the filler. If there are more than two pieces to the broken object, glue them together in stages if possible. Their alignment will be easier to control if you are only working with two pieces.

Small items can often be held in place by tying or taping them (with masking tape) to a support. Be sure the support or the binder doesn't touch the glue.

Repairing

Small chips can be filled and nicked edges reshaped with a mixture of plaster of Paris and white glue. Clean the raw edge of all foreign matter. This may require a little sanding. Have ready your provision for holding the object while the patching material dries. Mix the glue and plaster of Paris to a thick, even consistency—it should cling to a knife blade. Apply enough of the plaster to allow for some shrinkage. The mixture is quick to set up, so plan to mix and apply the patch immediately. Also, rinse out the container (old china cup, etc.) used to mix the plaster at once or you'll have to chisel it out. Allow the patch to dry thoroughly. We are of the "better to be safe than sorry" school and wait a full day.

Use dry sandpaper to shape the patch to the desired contours. Do not scrape off excess plaster—it will cause chunks of the main patch to break off. Work with a light hand as the plaster is quite soft and will easily sand to shape. You can achieve a final smooth surface by lightly rubbing with your finger tips.

For larger repairs on china—or anything else but glass—we use an epoxy putty. This marvelous stuff comes in a metal or wood tone. We've used it on dishes, figurines, and any number of other damaged things. It dries in one and one-half hours and cures, hard as steel, in twelve hours. You can mold, drill, saw, file, sand, and paint it. The product comes in two bars, one a resin, the other a hardener. To mix, slice off equal portions of the bars and roll and knead them together into a uniform-colored glob.

To use, dip fingers in soapy water and fill or shape products as required. To smooth out the edges, use your fingers wet with soapy water. The putty doesn't shrink, so shape and smooth to the finished size. If need be, use an extra-fine grade of silicone carbide sandpaper to smooth the edges.

The more difficult task is to paint over a new patch. You may have to blend a color in order to get the right shade. Old colors that have faded are difficult to match and call for experimentation. Be sure to choose the right finish—flat, semigloss, or high gloss. Apply the paint as thinly as possible so it will blend into the surrounding area. If the patch bleeds through the first coat, apply a second coat of paint. Overlap the first coat so the paint doesn't form a thick ridge. A small, soft-bristle artist brush will work for most touch-ups. The better choice is an air brush.

A standard tool of graphic artists, an air brush is a small paint spraying unit that allows you to apply a thin, even coat of paint. Professional units require an air compressor and are fairly expensive, but you can pick up a small, inexpensive unit in hobby and craft supply stores for around ten to fifteen dollars. Instead of a costly air compressor, these use an aerosol can of compressed air. When you run out of air, you just buy a compressed air refill. We have found that the jar (which holds the paint) is far too big for most of our projects, so we place a smaller jar with paint in it, inside the larger jar. When we're through, we just cap the small jar of paint and keep it for future projects.

CLOCKS

Clock repairing, as far as the workings are concerned, is a skilled profession. If the cleaning procedure outlined earlier or the replacement of the pendulum (if there is one) has failed to return the clock to working order, then it calls for professional servicing. However, replacement of the glass front, dial, and hands can usually be carried out by amateurs like us. Wooden cases can be refinished, and metal and plastic cases can be touched up to enhance their salability. Check a few price guides to see what your clock is likely to bring in good working condition. You may be ahead to just clean it up and sell it for less, as is.

GLASS

We run across a lot of mended glass, and with few exceptions it sticks out like a clown's nose. Most glass is transparent and a crack or mend is obvious, unless it occurs where the handle or other appendage is joined to the body or it is concealed by a design. Even so, many objects of glass that have been mended are in demand—particularly if they are crystal. Of course, their value is greatly reduced by the mend. But pieces such as those by R. Lalique can still bring hefty prices even when they've been repaired.

The edges of broken glass are smooth and should be scratched if you plan to glue them. Scratching gives the glue a better footing. You can do this with a rough-grade silicon carbide sheet. Just scratch, don't sand. Use an epoxy glue for nonporous materials. Apply the glue very thinly and fit the two pieces together as tightly as possible.

Keeping the pieces together while the glue cures is a problem. The pieces need support, but whatever comes in contact with the glue will also bond to the glass. We have had some success with this problem by laying up strips of one-inch masking tape along each side of the break on both sides of the glass. This means there will be tape on the top and bottom to the left of the break, and top and bottom to the right. Place the strips about one-quarter-inch apart for excess glue to run. This usually requires that the tape strips be cut in irregular shapes to fit the contours of the break. Place three layers of tape on the sides of the broken glass before you apply the glue. (The grand finale requires four hands!) One person spreads on the glue, fits the pieces tightly together, and holds them in place. The second person quickly places fresh masking tape over the break, bridging the strips in one or more Xs. The X binding reduces the possibility that the pieces will shift before they set. *Important: for the glue to be fully effective, it should set under pressure.* This keeps air pockets—voids that have no bonding ability—from forming. So for best results hold the pieces together for several minutes. After the glue has set completely, you can remove the masking tape and clean off the excess glue with a razor blade.

Cut and pressed bowls with scalloped or serrated rims (almost) always surface at auctions with one or more "teeth" chipped or broken off. They can't be replaced, but they can usually be reshaped with emery cloth, and thus be made less noticeable. Begin with a rough-grade emery cloth to wear down sharp edges and to shape a peak similar to the teeth. Follow with a fine grade of emery cloth or silicon paper and finish with crocus paper. (Glass is extremely hard and requires a lot of sanding to wear it down.) The glass will now be dull. Polish with jeweler's rouge (see pg. 144) or whiting until the dullness has all but disappeared.

Minor nicks on the feet and rims of glasses and similar pieces can be sanded out, as above, with a fine-grade emery or silicon cloth, then crocus cloth, and finally jeweler's rouge or whiting.

IVORY (SEE: BONE AND IVORY)

METALS

For the novice, the repair of metal items should be confined to the replacement of parts. Broken metal parts are repaired by joining the parts together with heat. Depending on the melting point of the metal, it is soldered, brazed, or welded. Although soldering can be done with an inexpensive electric soldering gun and many amateurs do their own soldering, we suggest you leave it, along with brazing and welding, to the experts (unless you've had experience).

PAPER

Paper goods that have a backing, such as the end paper of books, can be reglued or replaced without great difficulty. They can even be patched with matching paper. And if the paper has a busy design, the patch can be virtually invisible.

Torn posters and pictures generally can be repaired satisfactorily by backing them. Spray the backing sheet with an adhesive (obtained at an art supply store) and secure the original to it with a roller. Properly line up the tear edges and press into place. Use the roller to work out any air bubbles. If there are holes, patch with paper of the same texture and weight. After the glue has dried thoroughly, you can use poster paints or watercolors to touch up the tears, patches, seams, and other areas that bleed through your repair work. Spray the entire picture with clear acrylic.

To restore the gilded or colored-paper edges of books, rub on gold or colored restoration wax. Place protruding paper inside the covers and masking tape on the inside of the spine to protect them while you apply the wax. Let dry a few minutes, and buff. Soiled picture matting and similar paper items can also be rescued this way.

Wrinkles and creases can be ironed out of paper. This is not a procedure to use on first editions, historical documents, or other valuable papers (hand them over to a professional). We've used it on inexpensive paper goods that most likely would not have sold as they were.

Have sheets of blotter paper or construction paper ready. Dampen a sheet by spraying it with a fine mist of clear water. Place several sheets of dry blotter paper on a flat surface (kitchen counter). Lay the damaged sheet of paper on them and cover it with the previously dampened sheet of blotter paper. With an electric iron set to perm press or medium heat, iron the damp sheet dry. Immediately place a flat, heavy book or other object on the sheets until they have cooled. This will reduce the chance that the paper will curl. You can omit the ironing by placing dry blotting paper over the damp sheet and weighing it down in the same fashion.

Repair objects of papier mâché by gluing cracks and tears or replacing missing sections. You can make papier mâché by tearing up newspaper and soaking it in water overnight. Drain off all excess water and mix the paper with flour paste. It can then be shaped to fit the hole you're patching. However, wet papier mâché shrinks when it dries, so it is best to make the patch a little larger than the hole and sand it down to fit after it is thoroughly dry—two or three days. Glue in place.

Various kinds of mending tape can be removed by heating from the underside and peeling or scraping off. An electric iron or hair blow dryer can provide the heat.

POTTERY (SEE: CHINA AND POTTERY)

WOOD

The repair and refinishing of wood usually refers to furniture, but not always. There is a vast assortment of wooden objects in the antiques marketplace other than furniture. Walking canes and sticks, firearm stocks, carved figures, cups, dishes, bowls, trays, jewelry boxes, desk accessories, sandals, etc., etc. The basic approach to repairing almost any piece of wood is the same: repair the damage and return the article to normal.

White rings, which form on table tops from carelessly placed cups and glasses, can be removed by rubbing the spots with lemon oil and rottenstone powder (from a hardware store). To use, spread a little lemon oil over the ring, sprinkle rottenstone on top, and rub the mixture (medium pressure) in the direction of the grain. Actually, any light oil and abrasive powder such as a household cleanser will do. We've also used toothpaste. Wipe up the abrasive paste with a rag tacky with a little oil. Finish the project by polishing the spot and its surrounding area with wax, lemon oil, or a commercial polish. Use this method to remove any stain or discoloration that has only penetrated as far as the finish.

For cigarette burns that have penetrated to the wood, scrape out the blackened area with a pocketknife or X-Acto blade. This will leave an indented area below the surface line, to be filled with colored wax. Wax sticks are manufactured in several wood-finish colors and are available at (some) hardware stores. However, you can make your own from crayons and they'll be just as good (crayons are colored wax and that's what wax sticks are). Buy (or borrow from your children) a boxed set of crayons. For wood repairs you'll want black and white and shades of brown, tan, yellow, and red. You can use all the remaining colors to touch up paint nicks on just about anything.

To fill in the indention with wax that matches the existing finish, you need to blend wax from two or more crayons. Start with the brown or tan that is closest to the finish and slice a little into the top of a double-boiler that has hot water in the bottom section. Place it on the stove over medium heat. *Be careful: the wax is flammable.* Melt the slice and compare it with the color you want—to lighten add a shaving of white or yellow, then mix and compare again. For mahogany, you may need a touch of deep red. By adding very small bits of color each time, you should arrive at a match. When you think you have the right color, take the pan off the stove and let the wax cool—the color will change some. If the shade is off, reheat and add whatever color is required. Every time you add color, let the mixture cool in order to see the finished tone. If the mix is too far off, you can start again.

Fill the recess by dribbling the melted wax from a table knife or teaspoon. Lightly scrape off excess wax from the repair site with a clean, dull, table knife blade. Then gently run a finger over the surface to smooth, blending wax into the surrounding area. If the repaired area is not on a working surface, the patch is complete. If the repair is on the top of a table or where the patch is likely to receive wear, it should be coated with a mixture of one-part shellac and two-parts alcohol. After the shellac has dried for twenty-four hours, follow with a coat of varnish. It is best to apply varnish to the entire panel or tabletop—there's no way to blend in touch-up varnish. If the newly varnished area is too shiny to match the rest of the table, go over it lightly with #0000 steel wool. Finish off your repair with a coat of furniture wax or polish.

You can avoid all that work with the shellac and varnish by spraying a couple of light coats of clear acrylic or lacquer over the patch. Lightly buff the overlapping edges with #0000 steel wool, and finish with a coat of wax.

For any nick, crevice, or hole in a wooden object, follow the steps given above. If the object is painted, use a paint to match. For a finish with more or less of a shine, spray on a clear acrylic spray in gloss or flat.

Minor scratches can usually be concealed by simply rubbing with a crayon of a similar color. Shoe polish also covers scratches, but choice of colors is limited and application is messier.

Areas where there is no damage to the wood but the finish is worn through and the natural color of the wood is showing can be touched up with watercolors. Using as little water as possible, blend the colors to match the stained wood. Dab the watercolor on and when it is dry, wipe off any paint that spilled over onto the surrounding area. Watercolors dry a little lighter than they appear when wet, but this is no problem because they will darken when you apply a coat of finish over them—acrylic or lacquer, as described above.

Veneer that is missing from inlays, loose, or damaged, can often be repaired by an amateur. If the piece is just loose, completely remove it with a razor blade. Scrape off all the old glue from the piece itself and the surface to which it belongs. Apply white glue and position the piece. Provide the necessary pressure by covering with a weight while it dries.

If the piece of inlay is damaged, cut out the bad section and clean the old glue out of its bed. Fill this area with colored wax or paint to match. If the piece is missing, do the same. This unorthodox patching is not perfect but it should, if done carefully, eliminate an eyesore.

Many older furniture pieces, such as dresser sets, have missing or mismatched hardware. The desirability of such a piece, if not the asking price, can be increased by replacing or adding the needed hardware. You can scout flea markets for the desired hardware or replace all the pieces with a new set. Our personal preference is to replace with undamaged, old hardware. If we must use new hardware, we tone it down to look older (as described above under brass). This is not to mislead a customer; we just hate to see fine old furniture bedecked with shiny, new hardware—particularly glittering, new, brass reproductions.

Heavy ornate picture frames dating from the Victorian years, and the more delicate molded borders on pictures from the 1920s and 1930s, rarely come on the market without some damage. Most of the scalloping was done in plaster and glued onto the frame. The molded framing from the deco age was pressed into the wood. You can repair both kinds of frames with plaster of paris or epoxy putty.

The professional way to replace missing filigree and other trim is to duplicate the design by creating a mold from an undamaged section of the frame. To do this, you must apply molding material to the frame, removing it when dry. Then you must fill the mold with casting material, removing that when dry. The problem is removing the hardened materials. It's not a job for an amateur. We recommend that you opt for the simpler approach of fashioning the design replacement by hand. This is not as difficult as it sounds if the areas of repair are not too large. (Obviously, the smaller it is, the easier it is to create a passable duplicate.)

To give the plaster of paris holding power, mix it with white glue, as described above in the china and pottery repair section. Be sure the surface of the area to be patched is free of dirt and paint. Mold the patching material into the general shape desired and apply to the missing section. Do the sculpting with a teaspoon or whatever objects you have that will provide the impressions you need. (Sometimes this calls for a little ingenuity.) After the plaster or putty has dried, you can sand or file to correct and/or smooth.

Paint or use restoration wax to cover the reworked area. If the colors can't be matched, repaint the panel.

CHAPTER 6

Where to Sell: Cultivate the Art of Knowing

While a great deal of the fun (and sometimes frustration) is in buying, you're not going to make a profit unless you sell your merchandise. But don't leap at a market before you explore all your options. Choosing where to sell your merchandise should be approached with a great deal of knowledge and forethought. Even if you have the finances to go out and buy a thriving antiques or collectibles shop, don't do it if you are just starting in the business. A full-blown enterprise requires an equal amount of knowledge and money—one without the other guarantees failure.

Horror stories abound of retirees and younger enthusiasts, all of whom regarded the antiques business as a quick and easy way to make money but only managed to lose their savings. Over the last twenty years, we have observed scores of new dealers drop out or be forced out of the business because they chose an inferior marketplace or carried the wrong merchandise for an otherwise successful outlet.

Others failed because they didn't know the true value of their merchandise. So be cautious and begin in a modest way. Give yourself time to gain experience before committing time, effort, and money to this fascinating business.

A major plus in selling antiques and collectibles is that you can start up on a shoestring. The only investments you need are probably gathering dust in your attic or basement. The most common place to enter the business is through garage or yard sales. If you begin by selling unwanted household items, your investment will be limited to a classified ad in the local newspaper, so the risk of loss, other than time, is minimal. With the proceeds gained from one or more garage or yard sales, you can buy merchandise at auctions and other outlets. You can, in this way, replace and increase your inventory without investing additional money. We know several couples who have sold only from their garages for a number of years, and they are satisfied with the returns. However, most dealers move on to other outlets.

Outlet Options

GARAGE AND YARD SALES

Multi-family garage and yard sales attract more buyers than a single-family sale. Block sales attract even more. And community-wide sales (whole subdivisions or other urban sections) attract the most people. Our experience has been the higher the traffic, the higher the sales—other things being equal. Assortment of goods, their condition, competitive prices, and the weather are always important factors. We have a daughter living in a subdivision that has an annual community-wide yard sale. The one-day event attracts around eight hundred people each fall.

For the past several years, we have loaded our van with household items and other merchandise that isn't appropriate for our antiques and collectibles outlets, and have taken them over to share our daughter's front lawn on sale day. Not only have we done extremely well, but our daughter's success at the event encouraged her to go into the business. Now we have more in common with her, and even her children make some extra money by selling sports cards, electronic games, stuffed animals, and other unwanted personal possessions.

Garage and yard sales have become so popular that most newspapers devote a special segment of the classified ad section to them in the Friday and Saturday editions. Many newspapers sell garage sale kits with balloons and signs, or you can purchase them at stationary stores. A sign or recognizable symbol, such as balloons, is essential to identify your place of sale. Some localities enforce ordinances against placing signs on utility poles, others do not. The area we live in is inundated with poles bearing balloons, arrows, instructions, and dates of future, current, and past sales. Unfortunately, most of the dates are long past. Apparently, many people put up their signs far and wide but only take down the signs near to home. This is regrettable for buyers. Those bumper stickers that read, "I brake for garage sales," express the actions of a lot of people (the authors of this book included) who can't resist detouring from their original destination to follow those alluring signs. The outdated ones cause much disappointment and wasted time. So if you put up signs announcing your sale, please take them down when it's over.

FLEA MARKETS

Flea markets are usually the first commercial marketplace at which new dealers choose to sell. But novice beware! They come in all sizes, in all types of environments, and with all levels of merchandise.

It's a common misconception to think of flea markets only as depositories for dirty and broken discards. In truth, some flea markets fit this description, but they are only a very small segment of the thousands of markets found across the country. The typical flea market offers a wide variety of wares ranging in price from under a dollar to several hundred dollars, with most sales bringing the dealer between five and twenty dollars. However, there are upscale, authentic antiques flea markets where the average sales runs several hundred dollars with the upper limits in the thousands.

Flea markets are favorite fund-raising events for institutions, so you will find them in cathedral basements, college halls, school auditoriums, community centers, fire halls, parking lots, public parks, and cordoned-off streets. Revenue is raised either by having volunteers sell donated items or from renting out space to dealers. If the sale is open to dealers outside of the organization, you will usually find notices in the newspaper and on supermarket bulletin boards. Indoor flea markets of this type usually include a table for the fee of five to fifteen dollars.

Outside flea markets usually run a few dollars less but seldom include a table. An annual flea market that has proved very successful in the past may charge more. When you phone for information, ask if the spaces are reserved or assigned on a first-come basis; what type of merchandise is accepted; if a table is provided and, if so, what size it is; and if you can bring an additional table. And determine the set up time—is it the evening before the sale or an hour before the sale begins?

Privately run flea markets that are held weekly, biweekly, or monthly at the same location can offer you a wonderful opportunity to get a feel for the business. Hopefully your first experience will prove satisfying and you will end the day with more knowledge and money than you began with.

Our first flea market sale twenty years ago was a dismal failure. At 5:30 on a Sunday morning, with a second couple leading the way in their own car, we started off on a seventy-mile drive to a rain-soaked field bordering a country road in New Jersey. We split the twelve-dollar fee and the space and set up our card tables in the morning drizzle. Five other dealers eventually showed up to share the half-acre plot and the dozen or so browsers who trickled past our tables. Six hours later, without a single sale, we loaded our cars and sang the blues on the hour-and-half drive home.

We had met the flea market promoter at an auction. His lavish description of the property and excessive claim of high traffic had primed us with fanciful expectations. Those high hopes dissipated as the reality of our bleak conditions and sparse customer turnout became apparent. But we kept waiting for the onslaught of eager buyers. Our friends, who were just returning to the business after a hiatus of several years, explained to us that the pattern of traffic differed from market to market. Some were early morning markets, some mid-morning markets, and so forth. So we doodled away the hours anticipating the crowd that never materialized. That was the first, and last, time we set up anywhere without first investigating the location—but not the last time our judgment was in error!

It's not always necessary to actually visit a flea market to obtain the necessary information. Ask the dealers at auctions and other outlets if they have sold at, or know anything about, the particular flea market that interests you. Ask them about other flea markets they think are good. Question as many dealers as possible and tabulate the results. There will probably be some conflicting opinions, but there is safety in numbers. So if most of the dealers speak favorably about a particular flea market, go with the consensus. Be sure to find out what kind of merchandise the individual dealers handle at the flea market in question—it could be the deciding factor in their success or failure in that market.

A few years ago, we set up at an outside market where we had previously shopped and knew several of the dealers. We displayed an assortment of quality china, pottery, glassware, flatware, figurines, and the like. The traffic was adequate, the weather favorable, but our sales were wretched. The customers looked, admired, and moved on. We made three sales in seven hours—the biggest one while we were packing up to leave. Our grand total was thirty-four dollars.

The table beside us was manned by a couple who were in the business full-time. They set up at five different flea markets each week, attended auctions every night except Sunday, and repaired and cleaned up their merchandise somewhere in between. We were impressed with how clean their goods were but not with the merchandise itself, which included old (working) portable televisions, twenty-year-old radios (not the highly collectible early models from the 1920s and 1930s), electric coffeemakers and other electric kitchen appliances, assorted pots and pans, mixing bowls, inexpensive glass tumbler sets, and so forth—clearly not upscale antiques or collectibles. Their sales for the day totaled just over $300. It was the right market for them, but it was the wrong market for us. Although there are a number of reasons why merchandise can be wrong for an individual market, in this case it was the presence of fifty or more inside dealers at the adjacent antiques mall.

In the public's mind there is a distinction between outside flea market dealers and inside dealers. First and foremost, outside dealers are likely to be itinerant. They pay for their space by the day and, not bound by contract, are free to move on at any time. If there is a problem with an item of merchandise, customers may have no one to whom they can bring their grievances. Second, the outside dealer's veracity is often in doubt. It may be the American experience or just human nature, but people are suspicious of the transient—the individual who is here today and may be gone tomorrow. Third, the environment is decidedly grungy and a far cry from the milieu associated with quality merchandise.

Our inventory was similar to what the inside dealers carry at this market, but the buyers who were interested in that level or type of goods shopped inside. The customers who were picking and poking the outside tables were after low-cost, useful items. We should have been aware of this indoor-outdoor difference of goods at this particular market. But we had sold the same type of merchandise at several other outdoor flea markets where there were inside dealers, and with success. We had wrongly assumed all markets are equal. In sales, it pays to know your market.

Every market of any duration has a reputation regarding the kinds of merchandise it offers and the prices it brings. Here are some descriptive phrases we've heard from customers concerning various marketplaces:

"They have a great assortment of primitives, but the prices are too high." "You'll find nothing but t-shirts and junk there." "Big on oak furniture there—picked up a washstand in good shape last month, for under $200." "Lot of dealers, mostly Early American and English items. Prices are twice what I'd pay." "The place is a dump, but I've gotten some good buys on Depression glass."

Our first "permanent" outside location was at an antiques mall with two long pavilions, one on each side of the parking lot. Each has a high roof and a slab-concrete floor that provide a modicum of protection from the elements. However, most afternoons at about 1:30 the wind would change direction and suddenly blow across our tables in minute-long gusts. These brief, baleful blows often recurred for an hour or more. Unsuspecting dealers, new to the place, would watch their lamps, standing plates, and other high profile items get mowed down by the unexpected blasts. If one was quick and had two free hands, two items could possibly be saved.

Rain, when it came, swept across the outer fringe of our space, but there was usually time to move our folding chairs and empty boxes under cover before they became soaked. When we started in May, it was nippy at seven o'clock in the morning when we set up. And in August and September we had some blistering afternoons. But compared to the open fields we had sold at from time to time (and occasionally still do), it was (almost) paradise.

The mall's manager policed the merchandise of both inside and outside dealers. Modern household items and reproductions were forbidden, and the manager challenged any item he didn't think qualified as an antique or collectible. He was more successful in his enforcement inside with the permanent dealers than he was outside where he had to contend with the constant changeover of dealers and fresh setups each Sunday. A lot of taboo items were displayed—and sold—before they were discovered by management. But the intended restrictions did prevent the market from becoming a junk mill, and this was the reason we chose to sell there.

Most outdoor markets in northern climates close down around the first of November. Many dealers follow the weather and shuffle indoors for the winter—others follow the bears and other sensible creatures and go into hibernation. So our original plan was to adjourn the last week in October. However, we really enjoyed selling from the same spot every Sunday. Our inventory had increased and improved in quality; we were pleased with our profits; and—the real reason—we wanted our own "shop," however small. So we decided to take a booth inside the mall.

MALLS AND CO-OPS

Malls and co-ops are now the most common sales outlets for antiques and collectibles. A generation ago, it was the house by the side of the road. To be sure, the highways and byways of America are still peppered with signs that lead to private dwellings with a room or floor filled with treasures for sale. But these establishments are rapidly disappearing. Conditioned by supermarkets and shopping malls, the buying public prefers to park and shop where the selection is expansive. We don't recommend a private shop—especially for a neophyte.

Multi-dealer outlets come in all sizes and all shapes. They may be an old house on Main Street, a converted industrial building, a refurbished store, an updated barn, or other existing structure; a few are specially designed and built for multi-dealer displays.

Just as all cats are mammals but all mammals are not cats, all co-ops are multi-dealer outlets but all multi-dealer outlets are not co-ops. And then there are the hybrid outlets that are partly co-op. For the uninitiated, co-op describes the method of selling. Dealers either take turns minding the store or chip in to pay a third party to do the selling. The number of days per month a dealer is obliged to stand duty depends on the number of days the co-op is open each week. Two days a month is average for a five-day market. Usually people are available who will, for a daily wage, fulfill the obligation of a dealer who chooses not to sell. There are other multi-dealer outlets in which third parties, hired by the owner or manager, do all selling. These markets impose a surcharge on the dealer for each sale, usually five to ten percent. In non-co-op, multi-dealer outlets, dealers staff their own spaces and do their own selling.

The demand for indoor space is greater in the winter when the outside markets close down than in spring when they again open up. The first year we decided to take an inside booth, we set the target date for our move in late October. When all the available booths but one were taken by mid-September, we panicked and grabbed that last one. The both was twice the size we were considering. But we were fearful that if we waited we'd lose out at this market, and we were excited about moving inside. We talked friends into sharing the larger space with us and packed in.

The booth was sixteen-feet wide by ten-feet deep, providing each couple with an eight-foot by ten-foot area. What a joy it was not to have to pack up a dozen banana boxes at the end of the day, squeeze them into our sedan, drive forty miles home, and lug them up to our second-floor apartment. Our booth had air conditioning and heat so we did not have to contend with wind or rain. We had walls on which to hang pictures and mirrors and space for furniture. There was light—electric lamps for sale could be turned on, and we had spotlights mounted on the rafters, highlighting various displays. We were *real* dealers now. Customers were more attentive to what we had to say, and other dealers took us more seriously. We were having a ball and making money too. We joked that the rent money was simply an entertainment fee.

Six months later the same size booth directly across the aisle from us became available, and after the toss of a coin, the other couple moved over. We were left with half the necessary merchandise or twice the space, depending on how you view a half-a-cup of something.

We borrowed money from ourselves to finance new merchandise for the doubled capacity. Even so, it took several months to build up the kind of stock we wanted. The immediate solution for filling the empty spaces in our booth was to "borrow" furniture and pictures from other dealers with over-crowded booths. We didn't charge a fee for selling these items because the goods were not on consignment (we deal with consignment later in this chapter), and the arrangement was beneficial to both parties. As we sold the items, we replaced them with our own.

Sundays we arrived at our booth at eight o'clock in the morning (the outside market started an hour earlier) and stayed until five o'clock in the evening. The mall didn't open officially until nine o'clock, but dealers from other markets shopped the outside tables as soon as they were set up then moved inside when the doors opened. We often made half our sales before the official nine o'clock opening time. Some of our neighboring dealers who dragged in at nine o'clock or later missed a lot of sales. Many of these late dealers also roped off their booths around four o'clock in the afternoon. In fact, the slower the customer traffic was, the more dealers would go home early. It was tempting, but we stuck it out to five o'clock. And many a week we were rewarded with a hefty sale in those last minutes.

When business is good the natural thing to do is expand. Many dealers at our mall took a second (even third and fourth) booth. We chose to expand into a second market. Our options were limited to co-ops because our Sundays were already committed, and there were no Saturday-only outlets within driving range of our home.

We narrowed our search to a newly converted dry goods store built before the turn of the century. The owner-manager had done a terrific job. About fifty tiered-shelf units, measuring five-feet high by eight-feet long, were set up along aisles divided by display cases. Glass-enclosed cabinets lined the walls. Fluorescent light fixtures illuminated the entire space. There was a furniture room and an art room where dealers could rent space by the square foot. The place looked fresh and clean, but not sterile, and there was a broad range of merchandise. It was open seven days a week.

The owner was personable, knowledgeable about the business, and bubbling over with enthusiasm. He had attractive brochures printed up, was advertising in several trade papers as well as local newspapers, and on billboards at each end of town. As a co-op, the selling was done by the owner and a small staff for the modest fee of 4.5 percent. Prices were firm, with a ten percent discount for dealers (a standard practice in the trade). All we had to do was bring in our merchandise once a week, tag it with labels provided by the co-op, and arrange it on our shelves.

We were greatly impressed with the setup. The market had everything going for it—but one thing. It didn't have a track record. It had been open only a few months and there was no way of telling if the business would grow or decline. Since it was our second market we didn't have to make an immediate move, so we elected to wait three months. This gave us plenty of time to acquire more merchandise and to keep tabs on the success of several dealers we knew who were already set up there. We did move in three months later, and it has been a prosperous market.

LOCKED-CASE CO-OPS

It will take all your fingers and toes to count the waiting lists we've been on, and space has always opened up much sooner than we expected. There were two exceptions, both co-ops that housed locked glass cases exclusively. The owner of the first outlet gave us a grand tour with a lecture that lasted forty-five minutes on the advantages of his establishment. He said there were three names ahead of us. The wait would be two months at best. He'd phone us.

A few weeks later, we visited another all-case co-op. The manager of that outlet explained the setup, had us fill out a dealer questionnaire, and promised to phone us when a case became available. We never heard a word from either co-op. But we had decided against both co-ops and had not bothered to follow through with phone calls or visits.

We have sold merchandise out of glass cases. They are a shortcut to obtaining space in co-ops that have cases as well as open spaces. Having a case in such a co-op makes you a resident dealer; as such, you're on the inside dealer's list for space, which, of course, is ahead of the hopeful outside dealer's list. Most regular co-ops (unlike co-ops that specialize only in locked cases) have cases for rent without obligation, i.e., no duty days. The cases are usually locked, which is a great deterrent to loss from theft and breakage. The flip side of a locked case is that customers are reluctant to chase down a key-bearing salesperson. To do so creates a feeling of commitment and takes extra time and bother. Our experience, supported by several co-op managers we have queried, is that, other things being equal, locked-case sales run about fifty percent of open space sales.

In addition to, or in place of, the outlets we've mentioned, there are other places to sell antiques and collectibles—and without a time-consuming commitment.

AUCTION HOUSES

While we do most of our buying at auctions, we also sell there. We have found it to be the best way to get rid of items we can't or don't want to sell directly to the customer. Most of what we take to auction is merchandise that is undesirable for our outlets. Some of it is what we label "our mistakes"—articles that have flaws we failed to discover until we got the items home. Occasionally we put an expensive item that we haven't been able to sell on the block. But the majority of goods we take to auction are goods we acquired in box lots or in a lot with more than one item. We take out what we want and store the remainder until we have enough to consign.

Selling at auction does present a risk. Unless the items are high-ticketed and you place them with a reserve, they will sell—but perhaps not for a price you consider satisfactory. However, over the years we've been satisfied with this practice. The key is to be selective about where and when you consign your merchandise.

Auction houses differ as much as any other marketplaces in the level of merchandise they handle. The large upscale houses usually have auctions that specialize in one or more categories. For example, a few years ago we had an Italian tin-glazed earthenware istoriato dish from the late sixteenth century, with a pre-auction appraisal of $1,000–$1,500. We consigned it to Sotheby's, New York City, in February, but it did not go on the block until the end of May in an auction featuring "European Works of Art, Tapestries, and Furniture." There were a number of other early Italian majolica dishes included in the sale. In addition to this cluster, Christie's, New York City, auctioned off early majolica plates at a sale the same week.

The cooperation between Christie's and Sotheby's is for the purpose of attracting buyers from around the country and overseas. The larger the number of items in a compilation, the more serious dealers and collectors are apt to travel from afar for the sales. And, of course, the selling prices realized are higher than they may be with only a local clientele. These large prestigious houses will handle only the highest quality merchandise—don't bother taking in run-of-the-mill items.

Local auction houses usually save their better merchandise for special auctions, if the consignee is willing to wait. These special auctions may contain only coins, or guns, or dolls, or Oriental rugs, or another single category of merchandise, or they may simply contain the best of the auctioneer's current consignments. The more successful the auction house, the more frequent these special auctions. Most special sales are given wider publicity than the common garden variety sales in order to attract the highest number of buyers interested in the particular merchandise offered.

A number of auction houses carry on two sales at the same time. Oil paintings; furniture; collectibles such as Hummel figurines, commemorative plates, coins, or stamps; or humble box lots are often sold in a side room or outside while the main auction proceeds.

Selling at auction is always a risky venture. As a buyer, you have the choice of continuing to bid or not each time the price increases. When you consign, there are no more choices. The die has been cast, and all you can do is hope, pray, or use psychokinesis to influence the outcome. That's not to say you will lose money selling at auction. Just go in knowing that there is a risk. In some instances, you may be pleasantly surprised when your merchandise sells for far more than you had expected.

We know a dealer who started in the business by buying and selling silver pieces at auction. He would buy at small auction halls, polish the pieces and, in the case of flatware, would add a chest. When his expenditure added up to $400 or $500, he would consign the items to one of the better (upscale) local auction halls. He told us he cleared net profits of about thirty percent. He eventually moved his merchandise into a glass case in a co-op at which we were selling. In answer to our question as to why he had given up selling at auction, he replied, "I'm doing better here, and it's more fun." But he did have to wait for the right customer for every item. At auction, everything sells, and you usually get your money within two weeks.

To increase the odds of picking the right auction for your merchandise, attend as many different auctions as you can. You are probably already doing this as a buyer. But you want to re-evaluate them as a seller. Note the types of merchandise the auctioneer handles, how it is displayed, and most of all how it is presented on the block.

We have found that auctioneers who take the time to describe an item in detail and point out its attributes consistently realize higher bids than those auctioneers who just hold the item up and state that it is a cup and saucer or whatever.

Our favorite auctioneer has a positive comment about almost every item he sells. He generates interest in the most mundane merchandise by praising it. Holding up a piece, he'll say, "Isn't this a beautiful little creamer? It's pressed glass, but it looks cut! A few minor nicks on the rim, but they hardly show. This is a common star pattern so you can easily find a sugar bowl to match. . . ." A more important piece will get a bigger pitch.

In addition to having a good soft sell, this auctioneer cleans all incoming merchandise, with the exception of his outside box lots. Free of dirt, faults and virtues can be easily examined. And it's all out where it can be seen, not buried under tables or otherwise hidden.

He's so successful that we can seldom afford his auctions—most things go too high for us to realize a profit. However, we have no second thoughts about consigning there.

THE MIDDLE MAN

Another way to consign your merchandise is through co-ops and other dealers. Not all co-ops accept items on consignment, but those that do charge a selling fee of about thirty percent. They usually place consigned items in empty booths or cases, or wherever they will fit. There are a few shops that reserve a special area for consignment merchandise. Although the selling fee is fairly high, you won't have to worry about making the rent—a phrase that is part and parcel of the business. You are not under pressure to keep a particular space filled, as you would be if you were renting. And you don't have to spend any time either selling or setting up a display.

If you know dealers in shops or other outlets, you might discuss providing them with your merchandise on consignment. We have handled merchandise for a friend (a collector, not a dealer) who, from time to time, loses control at auctions and is in need of a bailout. The merchandise is probably not what we would have bought, but it is interesting and it sells.

Whomever you consign with, even a friend, come to clear terms on the selling fee and the selling price beforehand. Be sure to place limits on discounts and bargaining. The best approach to this is an agreement and an inventory sheet. Place the terms of selling at the top of the cover sheet. Along with the amount, specify when monies are due—at the end of each week, month, or quarter. Then list all the articles you are consigning in a column with the asking price beside them. Follow this with the minimum price you will accept if it is greater than the standard ten percent dealer's discount.

There should be at least two copies of this agreement and the inventory. You, the consignor, must have one, and the consignee the other. Such an agreement does not imply lack of trust, it simply prevents misunderstandings that often arise.

MAIL ORDER SALES

If you turn to the classified section of most trade papers, antiques magazines, and collectors clubs' publications, you will find a "Seek" or "Wanted" heading. Specialty dealers and collectors advertise for specific merchandise. There seems to be no limit to what is sought—airplanes to zithers with just about everything in between.

As an example, here is a transaction we completed a few months ago. A little over a year ago we paid one dollar for a bag of Lions (the service organization) badges at a garage sale. The badges were in the shapes of animals, states, air balloons, and so forth and had dates and convention slogans imprinted on them. We put them out in one of our booths and sold four of them for three dollars each within a month. Then they gathered dust for a couple of months without a sale, so we moved them to our other market. Interest was zero there too. The most appealing pieces had apparently already been sold. We took them home, socked them away in the auction box, and forgot about them.

Several months later, Joan was scanning the "Wanted" list in an auction trade paper where she found an ad seeking Lions paraphernalia. She wrote a detailed description of each badge and sent it off to the name and address listed in the ad. We had no idea what the badges were worth to a collector, so she asked for an offer if the collector was interested. She got an answer about a week later. It was her letter returned with $35 scrawled across it. Nothing more. There were twenty-four pins, giving us better than $1 each. With the $12 already collected, this sale created a $37 return on a $1 investment, less postage and insurance that totalled about $2.25.

Selling through the mail in response to a "Wanted" ad or instigating the transaction through a "For Sale" ad require the same follow-up procedures. Doing business through the mail presents risk for both seller and buyer, but there are prudent precautions that can reduce that risk.

First, the buyer wants, and should have, specific knowledge of what is offered for sale. The seller provides this by giving a full description of the item and, if necessary, providing one or more photos. (We use a Polaroid camera for this purpose—no using up a roll of film and waiting days for prints.) If there is damage to the merchandise being offered, it should be fully described and clearly shown in the photos. Repairs and the replacement of any original parts should also be detailed and shown in the photos. General condition should be given, such as: "like new," "excellent condition," "good condition," "showing some wear," "fair condition," "colors faded with some scratches," and so on. Of course, any of these variances should be specifically detailed. One-of-a-kind or otherwise unique articles are best photographed. However, a description of well-known items that are uniform in their composition and design should suffice. Collector series plates and figures, tableware, silver flatware, depression and carnival glass, famous prints, tools, and cameras are a few of the things that are easily recognized by maker, pattern, series, title, and/or year.

Second, agree on price and method of payment. Is it to be a C.O.D. shipment? Do you want full payment before shipment? Will you accept a personal check? Are you set up to handle credit cards? If the item is valuable, do you want a money order or certified bank check? Who pays for shipping and handling?

Third, pack well. Envision that box with your precious merchandise falling off a truck tailgate or a conveyer belt. You might also consider the probability that it will travel as the apex of an inverted pyramid of tonnage. If it's fragile, don't rely on wadded or shredded newspaper, use abundant bubble wrap and styrofoam pellets. They are lighter and the difference in postage should help defray the cost.

Fourth, get proof of delivery. If you send the package by United States Postal Service (U.S.P.S.), a return receipt of delivery costs $1.10, plus postage and insurance. If the package is insured for over $50, a record of delivery is kept at the receiving post office. If and when there's a dispute, the receipt can easily be obtained. United Parcel Service (U.P.S.) charges $1.00 for a returned receipt. Their ground tracking service, which will verify the delivery and signatory by phone, is 75¢. The information, if requested, can be obtained in hard copy (printed out).

C.O.D. charges by the U.S.P.S. are $3.50 for a value up to $50, $4.50 for a value from $51 through $100, and similar increases for values that exceed $100. U.P.S. charges a flat $4.75 for the service. In both cases, the fees must be paid up front. You can be reimbursed for this charge—along with the postage and insurance, if you want—by adding it to the amount of money to be collected by either service. If the bill is paid by check, that check will be sent on to you. If the amount is paid in cash, the U.S.P.S. will send you a money order; U.P.S. will send you their check.

Purchasing items through the mail is so common that many dealers use it as their major market. Certain collectibles, as mentioned above, are best suited for this market. Easily described items that can be listed in ads or in inventory lists are best.

We are acquainted with a dealer who has built up a lucrative mail-order business selling flow blue china. She runs small ads in trade papers and magazines asking collectors to send for her list. The list gives pattern, manufacturer, quantity, piece, size, condition, any special remarks, and the price.

ANTIQUES AND COLLECTIBLES SHOWS

Antiques and collectibles shows are one-time or seasonal events that usually last from one to three days. They come in all sizes. The small show may be sponsored by a local church, the super one probably is sponsored by professional promoters. The vast majority of shows fall in between these two and are most often sponsored by clubs and organizations. They are held in church basements, motel and hotel banquet rooms, civic auditoriums, sports arenas, or wherever the hopeful assemblage of dealers and patrons can be adequately housed.

Nearly all shows have an admission charge that ranges from two dollars to twenty dollars or more—theoretically this lowers the dealer's rent. Even so, rents are relatively stiff in comparison to other markets. Prices reflect the size, previous success, and the prestige of the show, and run from twenty-five dollars to $1,000 or more for two days. This explains why most dealers mark up their merchandise for shows.

"Important" shows are widely advertised, large in size, big in attendance, high in rent, and a gamble as to whether the dealer will recoup his or her investment. But this last is true of any show. The trouble with shows and extravaganzas (covered below) is that you can make a bundle or lose your shirt in a day or two. There's no time to average out the normal ups and downs of the marketplace. This is not to say a show is bad news for dealers. We know dealers who do no other selling and are making that bundle—over the long haul. There are shows where the sales don't cover the rent and expenses, and others, fortunately the majority, that are very profitable.

The bigger and better show organizers contract for the hall and book dealer spaces a year or more in advance. Some of them literally have three- and four-year waiting lists.

Antiques shows are likely to include some collectibles, whereas collectibles shows are specialized. That is, the entire show is usually dedicated to one type of collectible such as toys, guns, dolls, postcards, advertising, salt and pepper shakers, etc.

The atmosphere of a successful show is one of high excitement. The crowds pass by in waves, gawking, admiring, touching, and, sometimes, actually buying. It's hard to stay in your own booth with the familiar, when there's such a melange of the good and the beautiful to be explored. We take turns leaving our post to tour the hall. We talk to dealers we know and introduce ourselves to the ones we've not met previously. We appreciate the common, adore the exceptional, appraise the unusual, and assess our competitors' prices. We ask questions about particular items; about techniques on refinishing, repairing, and restoring; about antiques markets, auctions, and other shows. It's a learning experience.

The extravaganza is a rustic stepchild of the antiques show. They're sponsored by some of the bigger outlets with the acreage to support them. The ones we have attended—but not participated in—attract from 500 to over 1,000 dealers. The affairs we are familiar with are held three times a year. They run from Thursday mid-day, when most of the dealers are set up, until late Saturday afternoon. Dealers sell from their cars, vans, trucks, converted buses, or elaborate tents; on blankets, folding tables, stacking units, and infinite combinations of the aforementioned.

There are no rain dates so the weather is always a big factor. If it rains intermittently, most dealers stick it out. But if there is a deluge, the customers quickly take to their cars while the dealers fold their tents and steal away like bedouin tribesmen. We have seen this happen on a Friday, killing all chance for a successful engagement.

SELLING TO PICKERS

Picker is an unflattering term applied to a professional with a most interesting pursuit. The name is familiar to readers of Charles Dickens who described pickers on several occasions as culling through trash or the remains of the deceased for anything they could sell to secondhand dealers. Modern pickers are much more selective and sophisticated. In another field, they would be called brokers or free agents. It is an activity we would aspire to if we had more time and less aversion to traveling to large cities.

The job description for a picker is short and sweet: one who picks up only things for which he or she has a buyer. Tools required: a little cash, a lot of knowledge, and many contacts. Pickers sell only to dealers—well, almost only. If they learn that a collector wants a particular item and they run across it, they'll make a deal.

Following Confucian counsel, here's a picturesque illustration of how a picker we know works. Although he lives in New Jersey, he travels weekly to Philadelphia and New York City, making the rounds of all the antiques shop dealers whom he has cultivated over the years. He developed his roster by simply walking into shops, assessing the merchandise and prices, and introducing himself as a dealer who sells only to the trade. He would then offer to bring in properties in which the owner or manager expressed interest—with no obligation for their purchase. This clever and knowledgeable fellow continually updates his list of the merchandise each dealer seeks. This merchandise may be a specific item such as a Regency mantel clock or a Daum Nancy etched glass table lamp. But the request is most often for objects in a broader sphere, such as nineteenth-century Japanese cloisonné, signed Arts and Crafts furniture, or English sterling flatware made prior to this century.

Our friend attends auctions and shops at sundry markets looking for the best buys on merchandise he is (almost) certain to quickly resell to his clients. If a specific dealer doesn't need or want his purchase, one of the many other dealers he services will.

He has worked at developing a reputation for being fair and reliable. He knows how high a dealer is willing to pay for items; when it's possible for him to make a reasonable profit and still come in under the limit, he does so. (There's something endearing about the person who charges you

$50 or $200 less than you are prepared to pay for something.)

This picker spends a lot of time on the phone. He receives request calls from dealers and reports back by phone when he has located or purchased an item in immediate demand. He also makes regular phone calls to local dealers who may have what he's seeking. Many of these local dealers know the kind of merchandise he is after and will call him. This man has the advantage of buying in semi-rural areas and selling in the higher-priced metropolitan areas. In fact, we think this is the only way you can succeed as a picker.

We've sold to this fellow on a regular basis. When we were set up in a mall near his home, he went through our booth every Sunday morning. Neither of us has seen anyone quite as meticulous or cautious in examining merchandise and finalizing the purchase. He first toured all the booths that were stocked with the type of merchandise in which he was interested, noting certain pieces. Then he reappeared and closely examined those particular items, asking for the lowest price available, and then leaving. Again, he returned and re-examined the article, walking out of the booth in deep thought only to come back a couple of minutes later. Usually he paid our asking price, but on occasion he would say he could only go to a lesser figure. He was a good repeat customer who, we felt, was not trying to take advantage of us, so we would agree—even if it was for little more than we had paid. (Good will, like a good name, is more precious than gold.)

Many of the items he buys need to be repaired, refinished, or restored. Much of this work he does himself, but he recognizes his own limitations and relies on professionals for the more demanding improvements. This is always in his mind when he assesses an item and something you should consider also.

We were at an auction a few years ago and found a large, Victorian, quadriplated oval soup tureen, exquisitely decorated. The trouble was, the silver plate was worn down and large areas of the base metal were covered with corrosion. We weren't sure how much it would cost to replace, so we passed it by. We later noticed our friend, the picker, was spending a lot of time examining it. Sure enough, when it came on the block he was there to bid, and got it for $190. Several months later when the subject came up, he said replating had cost him $200 and he had sold it to a client on Long Island for $725, who in turn sold it retail for $1,100.

This was mind boggling to us—so we checked around to see how much it would have cost us to have the tureen replated. The best price we could come up with was around $400. Our friend was a repeat customer of a firm in Philadelphia and was, as you can see, getting the work done for about half price. Another factor was our market. Even with the break-even price of $600, the tureen might have become a permanent fixture in our booth.

Over the course of our relationship with this knowledgeable man, we learned that he has worked full time as a picker for several years and continues to support himself and his wife in a comfortable fashion. He is not only earning a decent living, but he's doing what he loves to do.

Outlet Options

Becoming acquainted with a reliable picker will give you a constant outlet for your fine as well as unusual merchandise.

We can't think of any other business that offers so many options of where and when to sell. Before you make your choice of market, remember that in this venture brains are better than big bucks—investigate before you indulge, and match your merchandise to your market.

Sales Strategies and Other Pointers

THE IMPORTANCE OF ADVERTISING

The twenty-first century is upon us, and there are still people who don't believe in advertising. As much as our mentality may be insulted by the parade of deceptive ads on television that vie for our attention, advertising does work. Each year, businesses spend billions of dollars on advertising for one reason alone—it generates more sales resulting in more profits than would be possible without advertising. Yet there are a multitude of antiques and collectibles co-ops, malls, and shops across the country that haven't gotten the word or don't believe it. Before you sign up to sell at a market, question the manager about the advertising program. If he or she doesn't advertise the market, then chances are you won't have good sales there. People don't frequent markets unless they know about them.

Back in the 1960s, Don wrote and sold advertising. The three answers he heard most were: "Business is so good, I don't need it!" "Business is so bad, I can't afford it!" "There's no need to advertise, we have a reputation for high quality at low prices."

Advertising will, if it's done properly, increase the flow of customers to any business. A good reputation is important, but word-of-mouth will take it only so far.

A few years ago, we scouted out a co-op housed in a charming ten-room, pre-Civil War farmhouse. It was beautifully refurbished inside and outside, and quality merchandise was attractively displayed. We liked what we saw and introduced ourselves to one of the two owners. Space was available, she said. In fact, the room we were most interested in was filled with merchandise on consignment; she agreed to move this merchandise if we wanted the room. It sounded great. We asked how long the co-op had been open, the terms of the lease, the selling fee, the days and hours it was open, and so forth. Everything so far was agreeable to us. Then we asked the pertinent question—where did they advertise?

"Ah yes, well, we're not actually advertising at the present, but I believe that is about to change. Money was rather scarce until I bought into the business, but now there is money for improvements and advertising. I feel very strongly that advertising is necessary, however, my partner has disagreed with me. But I do believe he is coming around."

We told the woman we'd have to think about it. Outside, we took a second look around. The house faced a busy highway; had a large handsome sign with the co-op's name; and smaller plaques that listed antiques, collectibles, primitive furniture, baskets, etc. The signs were, according to the co-owner, flush to the building because of a township ordinance. We had passed the co-op every week on our way to one of our outlets, for the nine months it had been open, without noticing it.

Several months later, we ran into a dealer who had shared one of the upstairs rooms at the co-op. She said she moved in when it first opened and had stuck it out for a year. She had spent a lot of time and money on furnishing her space with display cases and shelf units—to no avail.

Sales seldom exceeded her rent, and there was no sign of improvement on the way. Did they start to advertise, we asked. Only a one-line listing in a brochure collectively produced by local antiques markets.

Remember that little ditty: build a better mousetrap, and the world will beat a path to your door! Well, the world out there has to know about the mousetrap and where to find your door.

The name above the doorway of "Great Antiques" is only read by passersby, a majority of whom are not interested in antiques. Place an ad in a local or regional newspaper, and the number of people who see the name "Great Antiques" will increase a hundredfold, or even a thousandfold—but the percentage of readers who are interested in antiques is still small. Place that ad in a trade paper and virtually every reader who sees it is interested in antiques.

The moral of these two stories (we've a slew of others that would only prove redundant) is to choose markets that advertise. This is not to say any market that advertises is a roaring success. Advertising is essential, but it's only one important factor.

LOCATION, LOCATION, LOCATION!

Location is another major factor in selecting a market for an antiques and collectibles business, as it is in any walk-in retail business. Not only should the place be easily accessible by prospective customers, but it must offer merchandise or services that are in demand in that area. You can have all the proven ingredients, follow all the successful procedures, and spend a bundle on advertising, but you won't make it big selling air conditioners in Alaska.

Back in the mid-1980s, an entrepreneur converted the ground floor of an old textile mill into an antiques mall. The outlet is located in a city with a typical mixture of over 100,000 souls, some rich, some poor, and most somewhere in between. The renovation was well done; there is adequate parking; and a fortune is spent on running attractive ads in several trade papers as well as the local daily newspaper. The mall is open Saturdays and Sundays, and the number of dealers fluctuates between fifty and a hundred. There are well-publicized sales and other events to attract buyers, but the operation remains marginal. We suspect the owner has a tiger by the tail. He can't find a buyer and his investment is too great to just shut the doors.

With everything apparently going for this enterprise, why isn't it a roaring success? The answer—wrong location! Not the wrong end of town—the wrong town. When the first word of a new antiques mall opening up in the city hit the grapevine, dealer reaction was mixed. Most of our dealer acquaintances were excited—we're all looking for the perfect market. But a few of the older pundits shook their heads with an emphatic, "No way!" Nobody could give us a why, only a what: "The city has never been a marketplace for antiques. It's been tried dozens of times over the years, always ending in a bust." For some undetermined reason, that particular city is just not a market for antiques.

Choosing to sell at a new outlet always involves risk. Moving in when you can take your pick of spaces is enticing, while waiting can mean losing out on a good thing.

The problem is, there is no way of knowing if a new outlet will succeed or fail. Without a past record, there is no way to predict its future. The longer that record is, the more accurate it is likely to be.

Ask: are you required to sign a contract? If so, how long does it run? How strict are the rules of that contract? Do you have to give a large deposit? If the market is closed for a day due to inclement weather, do you still have to pay the rent? Contracts are okay if they're fair to the dealer. We wouldn't advise anyone to sign a contract for a duration of longer than six months, and we greatly prefer contracts that are on a month-to-month basis. In most markets where selling is brisk, month-to-month contracts are the norm. Management doesn't need to lock in their dealers. Dealers want to be there because they sell there. We've known dealers who've been stuck at markets where they're not selling for a year, all because of a contract. If you have doubts about how well your merchandise is going to sell at a particular place, don't sign a binding contract. Move on, you'll find the right market for you and your goods, and you'll be glad you waited.

Few markets are consistent year round. Every market we have been in has had both slow and energetic months. Some markets pick up during the holidays, others plummet. Sales for outlets in tourist areas usually rise and fall with the season. The day you walk in to survey the traffic may be an exception to the norm, or it may be the norm only for their super weekend sale.

To find out how successful a market is, ask the dealers. Most people are more than willing to share their experience and opinions if they are approached in a congenial way. We begin our low-key inquiry by finding something on which to compliment the dealer. It may be the display or a particular item. We then mention that we are dealers looking for a new outlet. Early on, we ask if it has been a good selling day so far. The reply usually provides us with a traffic norm. It may be something like, "It's always slow like this until around one o'clock, then there's standing room only." Or it could be, "I've never seen crowds like there are today."

With a few such questions, you can form a fairly accurate idea of what a dealer thinks of the market. However, you don't want a solitary opinion, you're after a consensus. So ask the same questions of as many dealers as you can. Disavow exaggerations of the occasional Pollyanna or malcontent before you arrive at a thumbs up or down for that market.

GETTING THE PLACE YOU WANT TO WANT YOU

Well-established malls and co-ops, where the parking lots nearly always fill to overflowing and the customers pour out laden with goodies, seldom have space available on demand. Interested dealers must go on a waiting list. You can sign up for the next available space, one of a specific size, or one in a preferred location. If you sign up for space and want possession in the near future, don't wait to hear from the manager. Drop by or phone every week. Remember, it's the squeaky wheel that gets the attention and the persistent dealer who gets the space.

Be forewarned that resident dealers have first dibs on a space. That nice little old lady with the Dresden china in the corner behind the pillar wants to move up front on the main aisle. Her space is promised to the young couple with mechanical toys set up on the lower (basement) floor. Their space will be available the first of the month. That space will likely go to one of the thirteen names on the waiting list.

Hang on, don't throw in the towel yet. Anywhere from six to thirteen of the dealers on the waiting list are not available or interested in the space anymore. That's right, half or more of the dealers on the lists have gotten sick of waiting and have found other outlets, are still under contract where they're now set up, or have just lost interest.

Here's a tip: if you know a dealer in a market that interests you, ask him or her to recommend you. In some outlets, a nod from a dealer will place you at the top of the waiting list. Managers want responsible dealers with quality merchandise. A second trusted opinion as to how wonderful you and your merchandise are is a powerful persuasion. This preferential treatment of a friend of a resident dealer is unwritten but in practice at many outlets.

CHAPTER 7

Exterior or Interior Decor: Set Up Attractive Displays

How you display your merchandise will have a great deal to do with how well it sells and what price it will bring. Many a customer passes right by a booth or table that may have exactly what he or she seeks because the setup looks unattractive and uninviting. You want your place of business to have the prosperous, intriguing appearance that will entice customers.

MAKE IT SPARKLE

First, regardless of whether you sell at a flea market, an antiques co-op or mall, your own shop, or are just starting out by holding garage sales, make sure all the merchandise you offer is as clean as you can get it. There is, however, a ratio of work to expected profit. For instance, if you have purchased a planter for a dollar and you anticipate selling it for three dollars, it won't pay you to spend four hours scrubbing it to remove the residue left by chemicals in the soil that had filled it. But it does make sense to soak it overnight and clean up the outside of the planter. Dirt can cover a myriad of flaws such as hairlines in porcelain, and a smart customer will probably avoid a filthy planter.

Some dealers refuse to polish brass or copper, theorizing that to do so makes the article look new. But there's no mistaking the lovely patina of older metals, and we always work them to the highest luster we can. Both dealers and retail customers want to purchase merchandise that looks its best. Not only does it save them the time and effort of polishing, but they know for sure that the ravages of age haven't left permanent scars.

Selling Alfresco: The Basics

BE PRACTICAL

The way in which you display your merchandise will be governed partly by where you sell. If the market is outdoors and you have to set up and tear down each time you're there, you'll need pieces for displaying wares that are easily assembled and disassembled and that can be transported with a minimum of effort. Remember when selecting tables, and so forth, that whatever you choose must fit into your vehicle. If you have a van or a truck, you have a fair amount of latitude on this. But if you're driving a small car, you'll have to be inventive.

Many outdoor markets provide tables. Some charge extra for them—others don't. There are flea markets where each vendor is given one table with the standard rent fee.

Additional tables are often available, but you must pay for them. If you're going to sell outside, it's a good idea to purchase at least one long folding table. They're available at almost any hardware store. The legs fold up, the table folds in halves, and the whole thing can be stored in a box.

If you're just starting in business and don't want to put out the cash to buy a table, then perhaps you have an old card table around that you can use temporarily. As a very last resort, you can use a tarp or blanket and put your merchandise on the ground. This isn't very professional, but it will get you into the business. To add to your display, you may want to use a tarp or blanket underneath your table. This works well for baskets, primitive tins and cooking utensils, tools, and other unbreakable, fairly large items.

In the outdoor market, you must contend with elements that you'll never even have to consider if you sell inside. Not the least of these is the weather. It may be unbearably hot or frightfully cold. It may rain on your merchandise and you, or you may find that the spot you've rented is located in a puddle resulting from a recent downpour. A wind can whip up, blowing dust and dirt over your treasures or, worse, knocking them over. Anticipating these problems and preparing for them will lessen their impact.

In summer, a beach umbrella is a welcome shelter from the sun. If you don't have one or can't fit one into your car, take along a regular umbrella. Some of the better outdoor markets have pavilion-type roofs. In summer it's wise to select a spot on the side of the pavilion that escapes the afternoon sun. In winter, position your display on the warm side.

Speaking of winter, if you're one of the brave souls who plans to do outdoor markets year-round, or at least well into the fall season, select your merchandise carefully. In some sections of the country, it gets cold enough to crack glass. Unless you're devoted to the outdoors, we recommend either disbanding for the cold months or finding a cozy indoor spot.

COVER TABLES

Tablecloths will set off your merchandise, making it look far more appealing than it will if items sit on a bare table. Hospital supply houses sell large, durable paper sheets that are used around patients' beds or in examining rooms for privacy. These are just the right size for most flea market tables, although sometimes it takes two to cover the entire table top. Or you may have a couple of cloths among your belongings. These will dress up your table, but make sure they look crisp and fresh. Sheets are another possibility for table covers. The twin size is the best fit. We recommend a plain color that will show your merchandise to its best advantage. Sheets or tablecloths with patterns tend to dominate, making what's displayed on them subordinate.

While a cloth adds greatly to your display, it comes with its own set of problems. A strong gust of wind can blow a cloth off the table or lift it up, sending your merchandise flying. Anchor the corners. This can be done with clothespins, thumb tacks, or tape. Then fold the edges of the cloth under the table and secure them also.

DEVELOP THE MULTI-LEVEL LOOK

You may want to enhance your display by creating levels. Depending on what you use, this not only results in a more professional look, depending on what you use, it gives you more surface on which to display your wares.

There are several easy ways to display goods on various levels. Small, square, or rectangular tables made of plastic are available at almost any five-and-dime or hardware store. These come flat in a box and have legs that fit into the corners of the table top. Not only are they handy to have, they're easy to transport and no work to assemble. Placing one or two of these on top of a very sturdy table gives you display space underneath as well as on the top surface. These small tables often go for just a couple of dollars at auctions. They come in a variety of colors. We particularly like the medium-blue shade, and it's what we used when we sold outside. Of course, at an auction you're not likely to have a color choice.

You can also create a multi-level look by placing the boxes in which you pack your merchandise either on the ground beside your table or on the table itself. As we explained elsewhere, we use banana boxes for packing—first, because they're a convenient size and second because they have cutout handles, making them easy to move around. But a banana box also has a fairly large, rectangular hole both in the top and the bottom, so we staple a piece of cardboard over it to ensure that our merchandise doesn't fall out. This also provides a nearly flat surface on which to display items. (You may prefer to pack your merchandise in liquor boxes—easily obtainable from your local liquor store—or in boxes from the supermarket. If the dividers are still in a liquor carton, it's great for packing figurines, glasses, vases, and other articles that will fit snugly into the sections. But you'll find these are more cumbersome to handle and usually lack the helpful handles that are standard on banana boxes.) To make the boxes more attractive, cover them with either a cloth to match that which is on your tables or some other type of attractive covering. Of course, you can only display unbreakables on these boxes. Put your delicate articles on a sturdy table.

DISPLAY PLATES SAFELY, ATTRACTIVELY

Plate stands add another dimension to a display. And since a plate stands erect in its stand, it doesn't take up as much space, allowing you to put out more merchandise. The stands should be placed well back on your table or they will be in danger of being knocked over by customers. And these stands are very vulnerable on a breezy day. An alternative is to place plates in a dish rack—the type used to place just-washed dishes in before the advent of the electric dishwasher. These racks hold plates securely and tipping isn't a problem. But they don't display their contents to full advantage.

AVOID ACCIDENTS

There are no sure fire methods to avoid accidents. But whether you sell indoors or outdoors, make your display as customer-proof as possible. Some people will handle your merchandise as carefully as if it were their own, holding whatever strikes their fancy tightly and firmly placing it back in exactly the spot from which they took it. Other people will go through your display as if everything there were indestructible, even allowing their children to pick up a precious piece of glass or china. They usually discard whatever they've been looking at anywhere they please. But even the best intentioned among us may brush against a valuable piece knocking it to the floor or the ground if it's too close to the edge of a surface. Low, inexpensive, or unbreakable items belong in the front, tall ones in the rear.

Some dealers put up signs that read "You break it you bought it," "Handle at your own risk," and other similar warnings. We're against doing this for two reasons. First, you want to be friendly to your potential customers—without them you're not going to sell anything. And these signs are downright intimidating. Second, it's next to impossible to enforce these threats. What can you do—tackle the person who is walking out of your area after just having broken your best hand-painted Bavarian vase?

TAG EVERYTHING

To put a price tag on merchandise or not to seems to be a problem for some dealers. Do you just put out your treasures and then quote the asking price when someone shows interest in an item? Or do you have each and every article tagged with your asking (not necessarily your getting) price? We tag everything, and we will not purchase from any dealer who doesn't. Of course, a dealer may overlook an occasional item and it shows up in the booth without a price tag on it, but we avoid the dealer who makes a practice of displaying merchandise without prices.

Why, you may wonder, does this make such a difference to us and to others who have been in the business for awhile? To begin with, it's a sloppy business practice. But more important, it gives the selling dealer the advantage of sizing up the customer and quoting a price accordingly. For instance, if a well-dressed woman comes into a booth, the dealer may ask a higher price from her for anything in which she's interested—because she probably can pay it—than he would from someone who appears to be of modest means. And if a couple enters the booth and displays an ignorance of the merchandise, a smooth-talking dealer can entice them into paying many times what any given, untagged item is worth. So it's our advice to price each item with a tag made out like the ones we describe in Chapter 9, "Take Care of Business."

Moving Inside: The Details

Indoor selling relieves you of the task of setting up and breaking down your displays. What a joy it is just to walk away after a hard day rather than face the task of packing up both merchandise and tables. As a result, you have more latitude in creating a semi-permanent display. You have several decisions to make.

USE YOUR SPACE TO YOUR ADVANTAGE

Do you want locked cases, unlocked cases, display pieces that are also for sale, and/or permanent fixtures on which to place your merchandise? Will you be selling hanging items such as pictures, wall pockets, calendars, mirrors, etc., or do you want bookcases, shelving, or display racks that reach almost to the top of your booth or display area? Will you be hanging lamps, bird cages, or other merchandise from the ceiling? Are you going to handle furniture or just smalls? Is most of your merchandise breakable, or are you into things like guns, cast iron toys, or sturdy primitives? And most important, how large is your space? Do you have plenty of room or must every inch count, so that your display needs to go up and down covering as much floor and wall space as you can? There's a lot to consider.

Let's say you're going to handle small furniture—tables, chairs, bookcases, knick-knack shelves, and items of that ilk. You can use them to display your smalls. And it would be a mistake not to carry any smalls and leave that good display space vacant even though furniture is your main interest. The use of small doilies or dresser scarves (also for sale) will protect the finish on your furniture pieces.

Now you must decide what to do with your wall space. Do you want to go in for a large number of smalls? Then you need shelving above the furniture, if the wall space permits. There are rules at every market that dictate what you may or may not do as far as marking up the walls is concerned. In some places, you're allowed to put nails, screws, or anything else in the wall. But usually the management will allow only a minimum of hardware.

In many markets, walls are made of pegboard into which you can insert hardware made just for pegboards. This hardware is either in the form of a hook on which you can hang a picture or mirror, or a bracket, two of which are sufficient to hold a shelf. We've not been able to find these special brackets deeper than eight inches, which is a drawback if you intend to use them for merchandise that's wider than eight inches.

Then there are strips of brackets that can be nailed to a wall. These strips have inserts for shelving about every half inch; these make for a very versatile display space.

There are the larger L-shaped brackets that you screw right into the wall. You put the shelving on them. These brackets accommodate much wider shelving—sometimes up to twenty-inches wide—but they aren't easy to adjust. Changing shelf positions means making more holes in the walls for screws. And unless you possess a perfect eye, you should use a carpenter's level when you hang them—something that's not as necessary with the other two types of shelving.

A small bookcase will provide three or four shelves on which to display antiques and collectibles. These bookcases can be had for a minimum investment; you can find them at auctions, secondhand or hardware stores. You can put a price tag on them in the event a customer finds them interesting, but make it high enough so you'll be able to replace the bookcase *and* make a profit. If you're going to handle books, these small bookcases are great for display.

Hollow doors set on sawhorses provide good, flat display surfaces. Used doors are inexpensive, and you don't need to purchase real sawhorses. There are metal clamps into which you can insert two-by-fours to make your own. You then nail the door to two sawhorses, making a sturdy, long table thirty inches by ninety-four inches. We have used this method a few times, covering the top with blue cloths and placing bookcases and the plastic, knock-down tables mentioned earlier on top of the door to create a more interesting display and to give us more surface. Since the cloth reaches the floor, there's great room underneath for storing boxes and other things that you don't want exposed. And for a beginner who doesn't want to put much money into display, it's one of the cheapest routes to take.

We have an inexpensive, reproduction bowfront china cabinet in one of our booths. When we purchased it, we had no intention of selling it, but so many people have wanted to buy the cabinet that we finally put a price on it and marked it as a reproduction. Should someone be willing to pay the price we're asking, we'll buy another reproduction and we'll have earned a profit. Meanwhile, the cabinet serves the purpose for which we bought it in the first place—it sets off and protects our merchandise nicely.

ADD THOSE FINISHING TOUCHES

How dedicated you are to the market you set up in, and how much you want to spend on the trappings for your booth or stand, will be deciding factors in how you decorate. We advise you to spend as little money as possible on the decor while still making it both attractive and a reflection of your personality. In one market in which we sold, a friend of ours papered one wall of her tiny booth in a pale pink wallpaper with a very faint, small design. She specialized in vintage clothing, and the wallpaper gave just the right accent to her merchandise. Since the wall was so small, she was able to purchase remnant rolls very inexpensively, and she papered the wall herself. The finishing touch was a pair of Victorian pictures. It was a stunning booth.

Another dealer hung a pair of drapes across the back of his booth. He screwed the shelving right through the material and every shelf had an attractive backing that set off whatever he put on it. This looked great for awhile, but the dust took its toll, and eventually he had to change the decor.

TO LOCK OR NOT TO LOCK

That brings us to the old and oft-argued dilemma—does merchandise displayed in a case, with glass between the items and the customer, sell as well as merchandise that is displayed on a table or shelf where a customer can readily handle it? The answer seems to be No. Glass cases intimidate people, and unless customers are very seriously interested they're reluctant to ask to see an item. So what's the solution? There are no easy ones. Nobody wants to trust a $400 vase to a tabletop where it's exposed to the brush of an elbow or the exuberance of a child.

If an item is expensive, or small and easily palmed, we keep it in a locked cabinet. The price is always readable through the glass, without having to remove the object from the cabinet. And we make small, hand-lettered or typed signs giving pertinent information. For instance, if a plate is Limoges, we put that on the sign along with the approximate date the plate was made. A Hummel would have a sign reading, "Hummel—full bee" (or stylized bee, or three line, or crown mark) and the name of the particular figurine. A sterling pitcher would have a sign identifying it as sterling and giving the maker. We make these signs on three-by-five-inch cards cut to twice the size needed for the message. The lettering is done with a calligrapher's pen on half the cut card. Then we bend the card in half and stand it up like a tent. We usually use blue or pink cards. Select a color that goes well with your merchandise. We have found that this method does help us sell from a cabinet, but the same item would still have a better chance of moving if displayed on an exposed surface.

Small, valuable items such as netsukes, medals, sterling articles, some Disneyana, and so forth can be kept safe in either a jewelry case that lies flat or a small, hanging, glass-front case. If you're in attendance at all times when your booth or shop is open to customers, you can keep this case close to where you sit, and its contents will probably be safe without locking the case. But if your market is a co-op where you have either a limited obligation to be there or you don't do any of the selling at all, you should keep your small, expensive items locked up. Whoever is on duty will, of course, need a key. In some co-ops, all the locks are the same and management has a master key. You can't unlock your own cases unless you happen to be on duty, because only those people who are selling are allowed to handle the key. In other markets, dealers provide their own locks and give management a key.

All expensive jewelry should be kept in a jewelry case. Or, if you only have a few pieces, you may choose to display them attractively in a case with your other fine items.

Costume jewelry can be shown to advantage on display trees made for this purpose. Most of these are covered in a velvet-like material. There are earring trees for earrings and standing racks for necklaces. Rings can be displayed individually in ring boxes or in a flat box made for the purpose of displaying many rings at one time. Another method of making earrings look appealing is to put them on squares of semi-thick paper. Cut into the paper about a half-inch on each side, slide the earrings through the cuts, and secure to the paper.

DRESSING UP DRAB FLOORS

If your booth has a concrete floor, as so many of them do, you might want to cover it with an inexpensive rug. There's no need to invest in a new one. Slightly worn, domestic Oriental rugs (which appear for sale with regularity at auctions), while not perfect, lend a finished appearance to a booth. Or you may opt for scatter rugs. Be sure that any rug you put in your booth is securely attached to the floor so that your customers won't trip. Rugs can be secured with nails on a wooden floor or with double-sided, heavy carpet tape on a concrete floor. You may wish to cover the floor of your booth with wall-to-wall carpeting. Remnants can be found for a song at carpet stores. Remember—dark colors will show lint and make your booth look smaller, and light colors will show dirt. A medium shade with a sculptured finish is safest. Whether you have a rug or not, you should have a small, hand vacuum cleaner to keep the floor tidy.

COVER UP BARE WALLS

A wall of pictures or mirrors gives an interesting look to your booth if it doesn't have floor-to-ceiling shelves. And mirrors are a wonderful way to create the illusion that a space is larger and less cramped than it really is. An inexpensive piece of mirrored glass will transform an old picture frame into a perfectly gorgeous accessory. Mirrors are great for other types of display too. An item placed on a simple mirrored square, which you can buy in any hardware store, will be reflected and show itself off to full advantage. And if your cabinets or shelves are mirror-backed, your merchandise will spring to life with an added dimension.

CREATE AMBIENCE WITH COLOR

The colors you use in your booth should be ones that best set off your merchandise. If you're dealing in tools, you don't want a pink background; and you do want something that won't show the dirt. Of course, you may choose to place the tools on the floor or hang them on the wall. You can then arrange other interesting items on your tables. Pink cloths lend themselves well to the display of fine porcelain or to very feminine items such as dresser sets, glove boxes, or perfume bottles. Black, especially black velour or velvet, makes cut glass and other plain glass items look spectacular. It also sets off rhinestone or diamond jewelry. Colored glass radiates on a white surface. Choose colors for your cloths that best suit your merchandise and have pieces of material of various colors that you can use to highlight special items. Again, remnants are a budget-wise choice.

If you plan to do shows, you might want to invest in custom-made cloths. They're advertised in most of the antiques trade papers. The cloths are made to your specifications out of an easily laundered, permanent-press material and are seamed at the table's edges so they fit perfectly. Most tables provided at shows are a standard size, and you can slip your cloth right over the table. These cloths can be made in a variety of colors, but most of them are dark.

GROUP MERCHANDISE SENSIBLY

As you set up your booth, either for a show or in your own market, you might want to group your merchandise according to category. This avoids confusion. Display all the collectibles together. Group the fine porcelain in another spot. Arrange glass in an attractive cluster. Primitives usually end up on the floor. This way a shopper who's only looking for, say, Disneyana will be drawn to your display of collectibles. This customer will be unlikely to give more than a cursory glance at the other merchandise in your booth. If you had a cute, old Mickey Mouse sitting in a corner instead of in a group, it would likely be overlooked and you would have lost a potential customer.

Toys are a magnet for children. And many of the old toys are fragile, their days for play are only echoes in the memories of former owners—yesterday's children. Over the years, we have found that it pays to put old toys well out of the reach of little fingers. Although parents should supervise their children when they are wandering about among someone else's valuables, many parents don't. It's simpler to remove temptation than to have the embarrassment of asking someone else's child to leave something alone or put it down. If you sell in a market where little folks are frequent visitors, it is even more important to keep all breakables as far away as possible from the edges of the surfaces on which they're displayed.

LET THERE BE LIGHT

The addition of a couple of well-placed spotlights will take the gloom out of most any booth. Some markets allow you to use them, and others do not. If you're lucky enough to be in the former, attach your spots fairly high up on the walls and point them toward your merchandise. The use of low-wattage, halogen bulbs will allow you to use more spots without overloading the electrical system. A light shining on cut glass makes it dance with sparkles, and it will sell much faster than the same piece sitting in an unlit corner. Aim a spot at a cabinet, giving a special, featured look to the contents. Or shine a spot into corners which otherwise seem dark and uninviting.

Lamps are among our favorite type of merchandise, not only because they're items almost everyone uses and needs, but because turning them on illuminates the booth. While we usually group similar items together, we make an exception with a few things, including lamps. Placing a few of them around the booth gives it a homey, bright appearance. But as with any electrical appliance, be sure that the lamps you put in your booth are safe to use. And if your booth is one you tend yourself, don't leave the lights on when you go home unless management has all lights on a master switch, as is the case in many co-ops and some dealer-staffed markets. Floor lamps are better in some ways than table lamps because they don't take up precious tabletop space.

We have a fluorescent light inside, at the top of our bowfront china cabinet. It didn't come with one, but Don drilled a small hole through the back for the wire and attached the light to the top back inside of the cabinet. (Remember this isn't an old, expensive piece. It's a cheap reproduction that we purchased for display purposes.) The light makes a world of difference. The shelves in the cabinet are glass, and the light shines right through to the articles on the bottom shelf.

While we're on the subject of lighting, you'll probably find that there are only one or two outlets in your booth. You'll have to make the most of them. Plugs with multiple outlets that fit directly into existing outlets in the walls will provide you with power for several lights. You'll probably need extension cords to reach from your lamps to the outlets. There may not be any way to avoid having an extension cord cross an area on which customers will walk. If this is the case, tape the cord to the floor with electrical tape. It's desirable to have a rug covering the cord, too.

The higher the wattage of the light bulbs you use, the sunnier your booth will appear. However, there are markets where you're not allowed to use anything over 40 watts per bulb. And in some of these places, if you plug in too many lights, the fuses will blow. You just have to see how it goes and strive to have maximum light in your booth at all times.

COMFORT AND CONVENIENCE

When and if you're manning your own booth, you'll want to be comfortable. In setting up your display, leave room for a chair to sit in. You'll also need a place for wrapping paper, bags, and your cash box. We've found that a very small table is useful. We have one about fifteen-inches round with a cloth that touches the floor. When we aren't right at the table, we slip the cash box under the cloth where it's not visible to passersby.

We also keep our paper bags underneath the table so they won't look unsightly. And the table provides a steady surface on which to write up our sales or rest that all-important cup of coffee. Next to the table, there's a chrome towel rack we acquired at auction for one dollar. On it hang sheets of plain packing paper purchased reasonably from a U-Haul company where moving supplies are sold. Alternatively, many dealers use newspaper to wrap up purchases for their clients. These dealers also use newspaper to pack merchandise at auction to move it from one market to another and to take items from home to market. We dislike newspaper for wrapping and never use it. First, the ink often transfers to the wrapped article, leaving the dishes that have just been washed looking smudged and unattractive. And, second, the ink gets all over your hands when you wrap or unwrap an item. This means you either have to sit in your booth with dirty hands or leave your booth to wash them every time you've made a sale. This is particularly problematic in outdoor markets where the rest rooms may be a good hike from the spot in which you're selling. And third, newspaper doesn't look very professional. If you want to run an upscale operation, plain wrapping paper is an inexpensive way to add that touch of class.

Of course, if you're in a co-op where wrapping is done at a checkout point, you won't have to worry about it except when you transport goods. For this purpose, we recommend you purchase moisture-proof bed and chair pads. Several companies make them and, as we mentioned earlier, you'll find them in most supermarkets next to the baby diapers. These pads have a soft inner lining that protects breakables, and you can use them over and over again. The bed pads are bigger and lend themselves to wrapping large items such as lamps and vases, while the chair pads are ideal for smaller articles.

KEEP YOUR MERCHANDISE INTERESTING

In every market there are the regulars—the customers who come through on a weekly or biweekly basis. Many are waiting to get in to start shopping when the market opens, hoping to find a bargain that's just been added to someone's booth before it's discovered by another treasure hunter. Any booth that looks the same week in and week out will be given a cursory glance by a regular and be passed by. After all, nothing ever changes; the regulars have seen all the merchandise—or have they? Chances are that nobody has truly seen all of the items in any one booth. But by rearranging your merchandise on a weekly basis the regulars and other repeat shoppers will eventually see everything.

You don't have to change your whole booth every week, but you should move enough merchandise so that by the end of the month almost everything is in a different position from where it was at the beginning of the month. Keep in mind that items at eye level are the most visible; give everything a fair chance to sell by giving it a turn at a prime location. Of course, you don't want to feature three dollar items in a locked cabinet. But you can move the neglected cider pitcher from the bottom shelf of the cabinet up to the middle or top shelf, replacing it with the Northwood carnival bowl that's had the spotlight long enough. And you can swap the picture, which has been partially hidden by a large vase, with the mirror that has been hanging in a prime position in the center of the booth's wall. Moving items also gives you a chance to clean them, for a standard component of all malls and shops is dust.

We caught on to the wisdom of changing displays when we'd only been in the business a few short months. We'd just switched a few things in our booth when one of our regulars (Anna, a lovely lady with impeccable taste and the wherewithal to buy what she wanted) came in and, spotting a few brass items we'd moved, declared with enthusiasm, "I just love those brass egrets, and I'm so glad I saw them before anyone else got here." We'd had them from our first day in business, but we'd never bothered to move them from the spot in which we had originally displayed them. All those weeks and months, Anna hadn't noticed them. She left, pleased with her purchase. She hadn't even asked for a discount. We decided to move things more often. We're still amazed at the number of people who will pick something up after it's been moved and say something like, "Oh, you just got this."

ACCENT HOLIDAY MAGIC WITH MERCHANDISE FOR SALE

Just as in any other retail business, people who shop the antiques and collectibles markets get caught up in the spirit of the various seasons. Some dealers choose to decorate their booths with small Christmas trees, paper Easter bunnies, large valentine hearts, or carved pumpkins at the appropriate season. While this adds a note of festivity, it also takes up precious space, and to most dealers space is money.

We always decorate our booths with items we have for sale and suggest you do the same. For instance, at Easter you might feature old papier mâché Easter eggs or bunnies or have a display of old candy containers sitting on grass (the type you buy to line Easter baskets). At Christmas time display an old nativity scene or figures from a creche, taking care to keep the price tag clearly visible so everyone knows they're for sale. Old Christmas lights, Santas, or tree ornaments add a welcoming note and are usually hot sellers. Papier mâché pumpkins or old Halloween costumes give a booth a seasonal lift. And for Valentine's Day, romantic pictures, nicely framed, suggest gift giving—especially with the addition of a small paper or cardboard heart inserted at the bottom of the frame. And, of course, old valentines are lovely and highly collectible. If your holiday display doesn't sell, you can put it away until the next year.

When we work a market during holiday seasons, we generally put out a pretty candy dish filled with wrapped candy for our customers. It doesn't cost much to purchase a bag of candy, and the people who frequent our booth seem to appreciate this small consideration. Next to the candy dish, we put a hand-lettered sign that reads, "Help Yourself and Have a Happy Holiday." Most of our customers are polite enough to say thank you, which breaks the ice. From there, they usually start talking about their interests in antiques and collectibles and often end up buying something from us.

CLOSE UP

If you're in a co-op where others sell your merchandise, you'll probably be responsible for cleaning your inventory but you won't be able to cover it up. However, if you're in a market where you do the selling, you'll save yourself hours of dusting and cleaning and keep your merchandise in the best possible condition if you cover it every time you leave the market—whether you're going to be there the next day or the next week. We find that old sheets or those surgical cloths we mentioned earlier are great for this. Before you carefully cover your tables and merchandise, turn on its side anything (such as candlesticks, tall vases, or figurines) that could be easily knocked over. During hot weather remove anything that might melt or be damaged by the heat. And remember that in winter extreme cold can crack glass, especially if it's old. If you've taken our suggestion and put candy out for your customers, either put it in an air-tight canister or take it home with you. But candy isn't the only vulnerable item. One Sunday morning we uncovered our merchandise, at a Sunday-only market, only to find all our candles broken and covered with tooth marks. It seems the building had resident rodents. From that time on, we've never left a candle in a closed booth.

We always close off our booth by putting a rope across it. This discourages anyone who may be in the building when we're not there from walking through our booth and perhaps disturbing our merchandise. Other dealers hang up curtains in a closed drape effect so that no one can even see inside. And there are markets that provide locked closures to which only management has keys.

Your displays depend on the type of market in which you sell. (We've tried to cover all the different ones in this chapter.) But whichever type it is, with a little effort your booth, table, or space can be among the most attractive there.

CHAPTER 8

The Fine Art of Selling: Creative, Common Sense Fun for Profit

"Business will be better or worse." That's what Calvin Coolidge, who was judged an honest president but no seer, predicted. We hope this chapter will help you realize the former.

The secret of succeeding in business and making it better is no secret. Have a throng of repeat customers and keep a fair profit. If you are achieving these two goals in your antiques or collectibles business, you must be doing it right. If, on the other hand, your business is faltering, you need to analyze the problem and make the appropriate changes. If you're just starting out, follow the advice of the 1940s Johnny Mercer song that admonished: "You got to accentuate the positive and eliminate the negative. . . ."

In every type of outlet, we know dealers who have quality merchandise, good locations, and successful neighbors right next to them. But their businesses are riding down, from bad to worse to nil. These unsuccessful dealers are continually amazed that other people are selling well "in such a lousy market." These people have absolutely no idea why "things aren't selling for them."

THINGS DON'T SELL?

Of course, that's the problem, things don't sell, they are sold. And these dealers don't sell. Some aren't too keen at taking orders for merchandise either.

We have observed them in action (or inaction) in every market in which we've been set up. Unfortunately, they are not rare. Undoubtedly, you have also encountered them. In varying degrees, they are unfriendly, preoccupied, uninterested, uncommunicative, and even discourteous. In the same way that there are animal lovers who don't like people, we can attest to the fact that there are antiques and collectibles lovers who don't like people. At least they act that way. However, it's more likely they don't realize what they're doing.

The modern, high-tech way to discover and correct personal behavior that is counterproductive to success is to video the person or persons performing the required tasks. This method is used to improve the performance of athletes, public speakers, and other business and industry workers. Unfortunately, the method is not practical for use in the antiques and collectibles marketplace. However, dealers can analyze their own selling techniques and particularly those of their partner—if there is one.

SELLING IS A POSITIVE SERVICE

Before we get into how to sell, let's deal with the morality of selling. Many people think selling is a nasty business and want no part of it. They believe that to sell, one must lie, cheat, and use trickery and force of some kind. True, some sales people use these underhanded means to achieve their end. It comes under the heading of pressure or hard selling, but it's not necessary, practical, or desirable. The soft sell is a more successful, far easier way to sell.

We're sure you've been exposed to the hard sell—sales people who have tried (perhaps successfully) to overcome your reservations by sheer argument. They wanted to change your mind. They pitted their will against yours and didn't care whether you could use, or wanted, their service or product. The end result justified their means. After it was over, did you walk away with a warm glow telling yourself, "That's a splendid place to do business, I'm going to tell all my friends to go there?" If you didn't, read on.

According to the dictionary, to woo is to invite; to entreat, to solicit. It's gentle persuasion! When this approach is used properly, the customer may or may not buy, but for sure he or she will leave with that warm glow, return again, and probably tell friends what a wonderful booth or shop you have.

WIN FRIENDS AND INFLUENCE CUSTOMERS

Consciously determine that you are going to do all you can to convert every visitor to your booth into a repeat customer. How do you do this? You play the gracious host. To begin with, don't stand at the entrance of your booth with folded arms. That's hostile body language. If you're not busy with another customer, greet new arrivals with a smile, a "Hi, how are you today," or other friendly words. If you are busy, at the very least give them a smile. That's obvious, you say. Yes, but it's easily and often forgotten or ignored.

We visit so many shops and booths where the attendant fails to look up, or silently nods, or mutters something in a deadpan, monotone voice. Responses of this nature make us feel like we're intruding upon and annoying the so-called salesperson.

One time we had a booth across from two sisters who often failed to sell enough to cover their rent. The older, who had a less than winning personality, sold pretty well. But her sister, who was very pleasant, seldom sold anything. The sisters took turns staffing the booth, and one would stay while the other wandered around. Unfortunately, the older sister was gone more than the younger sister who would sit in the corner and read—a paper, a book, a magazine, anything. She never looked up when a customer came into the booth. If the customer walked past her, she would pull in her feet without missing a word of what she was reading. If somebody asked a question, she would look up and answer it—without any interest. Hence, these sisters had very few sales.

The world of antiques is small, and we were once set up near the sisters at a show. The younger one had her nose in a book there too, and their booth had less action than a mausoleum.

FORGET YOUR TROUBLES

Eliminate the negative, all of it. Don't cry the blues, complain about the economy, or knock your competitors within shouting distance of a customer. This kind of dialogue creates a downdraft. Cold air sinks and warm air rises. You want to uplift your customer, not so much because you're a wonderful person, but because people are more apt to buy when their spirits are high. Such talk is not only a turnoff for the moment, but it registers in the customer's brain as a negative smudge to forever be associated with you.

We know a dealer who is a chronic complainer. Although she has excellent taste in merchandise and always has a number of unusual items, she's always in arrears in her rent. We've overheard her tell customers that an item in question has come from her own house and that she is selling it because she needs the money. Even when she makes a fairly large sale, she's unhappy. "I didn't sell it, I gave it away!" is her frequent retort when we congratulate her on selling a particularly nice item.

We've observed her discussing personal problems in a clearly audible voice with the dealer next to her and in front of a slew of passing customers. And we've witnessed frowns on those customers' faces. Unfortunately, her sales are few. Her negativity breeds distrust.

In selling, as in most other human encounters, it's not only what you say and do, but how you say it and do it. Frank Betcher pointed out, in his classic book *How I Raised Myself from Failure to Success in Selling,* that enthusiasm is the all-important ingredient in successful selling.

It was, he wrote, the single factor that brought him success and wealth. Betcher wasn't the first, or last, to emphasize the necessity of coloring the sales message with positive emotions.

Emotion is contagious. It's an inner feeling that manifests itself through physical changes and movements that observers subconsciously read and internalize. Gestures, facial expressions, and tone of voice convey emotion, vapid words do not.

A young single mother who had a booth next to us in a mall a few years ago had never read Betcher's book. But she bubbled over with enthusiasm in her every word and movement when a customer showed interest in any of her merchandise. On one occasion, an elderly woman was looking at a tapestry hanging in our booth, when the young woman walked up beside her and silently appraised the article for a moment.

"Isn't that a lovely scene," she said with admiration on her face and in her voice. "The figures are so graceful, so well done . . . the man and woman are obviously in love, don't you think?"

The older woman peered closer, "Yes, yes you must be right," she said with new appreciation.

"And the small roses," our friend continued, "notice the details, the little thorns, the delicate shading—it boggles the mind to think of how much thought and work must have gone into its creation." She reached over and gently stroked the tapestry, "It's definitely very old, yet it's in such beautiful condition—I just love it!"

"It is very lovely," the customer enthused as she backed

away to a broader vantage point. "Yes, it's very lovely. How much is it?"

Our dealer friend leaned over and read the price tag. She shook her head in astonishment, "I can't believe it, they're only asking ninety-five dollars. Why, one similar to this, but very worn, went for $140 at auction two weeks ago."

The customer set down her plastic shopping bag and pulled up a corner of the tapestry to examine the back. "It is in good condition . . . I don't know, I've just had my dining room painted and I was thinking of replacing an old mirror over my sideboard with a new one. The tapestry would just fit, but perhaps it's too dark."

"What color are the walls now?"

"A light pink."

"Like the pink of the ribbon around the girl's waist?" our friend asked.

The woman studied the ribbon. "Yes, or very close to that."

The dealer clasped her hands together in joy and exclaimed, "Wonderful! It's meant for you. Countless people have admired it today, but they were blocked from buying it."

The customer gave a nervous smile, to which our neighbor replied, "It's true, we have an affinity for certain things and people, and we're brought together with them. This tapestry was meant for you the moment you decided to replace the mirror."

The older woman said thoughtfully, "You could be right, sometimes it looks that way. I don't know if a tapestry fits into that category, but I do like it, and I'm thinking it is just the thing for over the sideboard.

"I know you'll be pleased with it for years to come," our super saleswoman said to the customer as she strolled out of the booth.

EASY DOES IT

People don't like to be ignored, but more than that, they don't like to be hounded, so don't follow them like a shadow. Advise the customer in a warm tone of voice that you will be happy to answer any questions or retrieve any items locked up or beyond their reach. When a customer shows particular interest in an article by holding it up or studying it from different angles, it's useful to offer information: "Isn't that a beautiful old crystal pitcher? The copper-wheel cut pattern suggests art nouveau. There is a very tiny nick here at the base of the applied handle—see, it's hardly noticeable. After seventy or so years, it's a wonder there isn't some serious damage." The customer nods and looks elsewhere—the signal for lost interest. You smile, and lovingly replace the pitcher. The customer moves on through the booth, and you return to other things while keeping an eye peeled for the need of further assistance.

If the customer begins to leave without a purchase, you may ask if he or she is looking for anything special. If the answer is, "No, just looking," then say thank you for visiting your booth and mention that your merchandise is always changing; invite the customer to come back to browse again.

This particular scenario took place in our booth. It was typical of a thousand no-sale encounters we have had. Its ending is also typical. Two weeks later the customer returned and asked for the pitcher. She said the pitcher was very similar to one that had belonged to her mother, and it had triggered childhood memories of her farm life in the 1940s. This woman had become so excited about the pitcher and wanted it so badly, that (we joked later) she might have become violent if it had been sold to someone else. She still comes in about once a month and usually makes a purchase.

YOU DEAL IN TREASURES

Every item in your booth should be valuable. Refer to it and treat it as such. Beauty (as well as utility and interest) is in the eye of the beholder. The most humble item has praiseworthy qualities. Find them and point them out to your customers. If you can't identify a positive quality, chuck that item into your auction box. You can't sell worthless things.

We tried a half-price table, where we literally marked existing prices in half. It was not a roaring success. Some people believed the prices had been increased in order to mark them down. Others acted like everything on the table was inferior. We did sell fifty or so items in two months of Sundays, but we decided that selling at cost was not for us. We both had the impression that the sale table cheapened the booth. But that's only the experience of one couple, one time, in one market.

PRICE IT RIGHT

The marketplace psychology exhibited in antiques and collectibles outlets is different from other United States markets. While customers didn't exert themselves gobbling up the goodies on our half-price table, most of them expect to bargain for a better price. There are a few who are reluctant to ask, "Is this your best price?" or "Can you do better?" But those few are more than compensated for by the many who are never satisfied with the reduced price offered.

In pricing you must, of course, take into consideration the fact that you'll be negotiating prices. We seldom come down on anything marked five dollars or less. On higher priced goods, we allow a ten percent or more discount, depending on the price we paid for the merchandise. The average markdown is around fifteen percent. There are items where there is little latitude for a discount, and we simply tell the customer we're sorry, but it's the best we can do.

Every large co-op we have been in, or heard of, sells merchandise at the prices as marked to the general public, with no dickering. They do, however, give dealers who have sales tax numbers a ten percent courtesy discount. This discount is often limited to items priced over a minimum, such as five dollars. Smaller co-ops run by one or two individuals may want the freedom to lower prices from ten to twenty-five percent in order to make a sale. Dealers must mark their goods with this in mind.

It has been said that most merchandise is turned over four times before it comes to rest in a customer's home. In other words, dealers buy from dealers. We sell about seventy percent of our merchandise to other dealers. To do this, we keep our prices as low as possible. We don't sacrifice our margin of profit, we simply place a lower ceiling on how much we will pay for something. This approach handicaps us when competing against high bidders, and we have to cover more ground to acquire the necessary merchandise. But the additional sales are worth it to us. Some dealers sell only to retail customers. They wait longer for sales, but they get more money for their merchandise. You need to know where you fit into the market.

ADD PROFITS: CLEAN IT

Keep everything clean—there should be no need to pass out paper towels. There are too many dealers around who seem to think dirt is an inviting plus. Rust and filth enhance precious few things. We take everything home from the auction or outlet and wash and clean it. We find far more hidden beauty than flaws. Clean items sell more quickly, and at higher prices.

Last year we bought a five-candle electric hanging fixture from an outside dealer. This fellow cleans—no, empties—out attics and basements, throws the potpourri of stuff into his open-bed truck, and hauls it to market in its pure, untouched, as found, condition. The fixture had what looked to be a century of grime layered on it, but it was circa 1930. The dealer wanted $35 for it, said he'd take $25, and accepted $18.

With a little elbow grease aided by Fantastik™, we scrubbed away the years and found the original bronze-colored finish with a blue and red incised design. We also found the patent date of 1927. There was no serious damage, only some minor scratching and chipping of the finish. We elected not to touch it up or replace the original wiring. With a price of $130, it sold in about two weeks.

HONESTY IS THE BEST POLICY

Don't misrepresent your merchandise. Remember what Lincoln (who had considerably more smarts than Coolidge) said about fooling people: "It is true that you may fool all the people some of the time; you can even fool some of the people all the time; but you can't fool all of the people all the time."

Unfortunately, there are dealers out there who take exception to Lincoln's words and believe you can fool everybody all the time. They give the business a reputation that equates selling antiques with chicanery. These dealers aren't bona fide forgers, they're just liars. When we hear about one of them getting caught, we have a quiet celebration at home.

Other dealers can help you to sell goods with which they're more familiar than you are. We recently had a very profitable experience with this type of sale. A pair of original oils by a well-known twentieth-century American artist, failed to make the minimum bid at an auction we attended. We cornered the auctioneer after the sale and made an offer of less than the minimum. The next day the auctioneer contacted the consignor who refused our offer, but said he would sell the paintings at the reserved price. We agreed.

During the three or four days of these negotiations, we created a partnership, limited to this purchase, with a knowledgeable and trusted friend. He knew far more than we did about art and had a number of contacts for selling paintings. He examined the oils with a black light and located several places where one of the paintings had been touched up—not visible under normal light. However, such minor repairs are not uncommon on oils that are a hundred years old or more.

Within hours of closing the deal with the auctioneer, our friend phoned a dealer who, in turn, contacted a collector with whom he had done a lot of business. The dealer paid us cash for the oils, marked the asking price up, and sold them to the collector. Everybody was happy. We had made several thousand, the middle dealer had made a few thousand, and the collector had acquired important paintings at far less money than they would have cost in a major market.

MAKE A LIST OF CUSTOMER WANTS

One of the most successful ways to guarantee repeat customers and generate sales is to record the wants of collectors and other buyers. Whenever possible, we jot down their names, phone numbers, and the items they collect or seek. Many serious collectors have business cards printed with this information. We try to establish a price range and other limiting factors concerning this merchandise. Often collectors are interested only in certain classifications of their speciality, such as Occupied Japan tea cups, Black salt and pepper sets, art deco smoking accessories, or pre-World War II Hummel figures.

We buy only items, collectibles, or general merchandise that we believe we can sell elsewhere. That is, we try to avoid investing in an item in which only one of our customers may be interested. If for some reason the original customer doesn't want it—they have one like it; they bought one somewhere else; it's not quite what they had in mind—we don't want to be stuck with it.

If and when we locate a wanted item, we phone the customer, even if they frequent our booth on a weekly basis. This helps reduce the possibility of their picking up the article from another dealer.

Some collectors will ask if you have any of what they collect, others will not. While the general merchandise buyer browses through a booth, collectors usually scan, looking only for their one interest. And they develop an uncanny ability to spot their desired item.

In our early days in the business when we were selling outside, we bought a box lot that contained a particular piece we wanted. Included among the remaining junk was a toy motorcycle of molded plastic. It measured about three inches long and had faded to the bland color of wet sand. It was not a candy container, which is a popular collectible. It's doubtful that it had cost more than a dime in the previous decade or so when it was first sold. We had intended to throw it out, but it had inadvertently ended up in one of our banana crates at the market. We ran across it during our unpacking and tossed it into an open box under a table at the rear of our space.

We noticed a man in a black leather jacket zipping through the various spaces across the aisle from us. In time, he made it to our tables and with hardly a pause rushed to the back of the stall and picked out the motorcycle. With an expression that says "Eureka!" he cried, "How much?"

Now, we firmly believe the seller should set the price, but we didn't have the foggiest notion of its worth. When we can't find a listing for some obscure item, we ask several other dealers what they think it's worth. There's usually a wide variance in the replies, and we go for a price a little below the mean. We hadn't done this with the motorcycle because, in our eyes, it was worthless.

The young man stood there waiting for a reply. Don stood there with a dumb look on his face. "I'm not sure, we haven't had a chance to price it yet. What's it worth to you?"

"Ah, two dollars?" the customer questioned.

Don shook his head, "That's outlandish. Let's make it a dollar."

"Great," the leather jacket answered with a big grin. "I collect motorcycle stuff—all kinds, any kind."

"What's so special about this motorcycle?" Don asked.

"I didn't have one like it," was the reply.

Serious collectors are infected with a compulsion that equals that of severely addicted drinkers or gamblers. Even when the economy is in a slump and other markets are stalled, the collector is out there buying his or her heart's desire. Take advantage of this fact and, when possible, pick up some of the collectibles that are selling well.

KNOW YOUR MERCHANDISE

We've said it before and we'll say it again, knowledge is essential in this business. The more you know the wiser you can buy, and the easier it is to sell. As stated elsewhere in this book, the field of antiques and collectibles is so great that no one (with the exception of the fictional English antiques dealer, Lovejoy) can know everything there is to know about all the general branches such as art, arms, baskets, dolls, jewelry, mechanical toys, optical instruments, pottery, etc., etc., let alone all the minor divisions and all their individual examples.

You will never need to know everything about the business. However, you do need to know everything you can about the merchandise you handle. If you're going to sell Oriental antiques, then you'd better bone up on the different objects, their countries of origin, their history, material, marks, uses, and values. The same is true for other collectibles and general merchandise.

Ignorance about an item usually causes a dealer to pay too much for it and, in turn, price it too high or too low. A dealer will then also lack information to inform the buyer on the item's attributes, uniqueness, and desirability. In addition, out of ignorance many items are mislabeled. To a knowledgeable buyer this can indicate, at the very least, greenness. To an innocent buyer, it can mean putting out good money for the wrong item. Neither finale encourages repeat patronage.

It's impossible to name all the items or period styles that are mislabeled, but it should be of help to clarify the difference between art nouveau and art deco, the two styles we have most often found confused.

Art nouveau dates from the early 1890s to 1930. Its

theme was nature, characterized by sinuous, flowing lines and floral forms. Art nouveau women are depicted nude or in long graceful gowns, and their hair is long and luxurious.

Art deco was initiated in 1925 and lasted through the 1940s. It reflected industry and machines—*modern* and *streamline* are two words that describe art deco. Less expensive items are made of chrome, plastic, and pot metal; higher priced items are found in silver and ivory. Lines are straight and bold. Forms are often sleek, suggesting speed. Art deco women are usually depicted in revealing tights, short skirts, or nude. Their hair is cut short.

SELLING DIRECTLY

If you develop the skill and have the time, choose a market where you can sell directly rather than a market where your merchandise is sold for you. Other things being equal—right market, right merchandise, right pricing—you will realize more profit from a table or booth that you staff yourself. The enthusiasm and knowledge you can provide the customer is lacking in the supermarket-type co-op. If you are at all sociable, the real enjoyment in this business is meeting people and sharing your knowledge and merchandise with them. It really is rewarding to watch a customer waltz out of your space, excited about a newly obtained treasure.

CHAPTER 9

Take Care of Business: You'll Be Glad You Did

While this is a fun business, it is a business, and you must take care of all the pesky details involved in any vocation.

WHAT'S IN A NAME?

Your first consideration may well be to select a name for this new venture of yours. We've seen any number of cute and clever names such as "Grandma's Attic," "Hidden Treasures," "Yesteryear," "Memories," and the like. But the trouble with these names and others like them is that you have to pay to register them in most states. And how many people want to start a business by shelling out cash before they've even begun to take in money?

In Pennsylvania, for instance, you have to register the name with the state and then pay to have the registration of the name printed in the paper. You can, however, use your own last name without paying a fee. Our business is called Bingham's Antiques and Collectibles. We could have used Don and Joan Bingham's Antiques and Collectibles, without being required to register it. But had we opted for Don and Joan's Antiques and Collectibles, we'd have been obliged to notify the state of Pennsylvania and the newspaper and pay our fee. To find out the rules for your state call your state department of commerce or economic affairs.

TAX NUMBERS: FIRST THINGS FIRST

In most states, you'll need a tax number. You can get one by applying to the state's department of revenue. They'll send you a document with your tax number on it. Carry it with you and post a copy of it in the place where you sell.

This number permits you to buy at auction and other outlets without paying a state sales tax. The reasoning behind this is that you're buying for resale and, therefore, your purchases are legitimate business expenses. The state gets its share when you tax your customers. When you sign up for a bidding number at an auction, show your tax number. If you fail to do this, you'll be charged the state tax when you check out of the auction.

You may use your tax number when you buy anything for your business—anything that you're going to resell, that is. For instance, if, at the local hardware store, you purchase a mirror to go into an antique frame you're planning to sell, you can show the clerk your number and you won't be charged sales tax. However, if you buy a computer on which to keep your records, you must pay sales tax on it because you're planning to keep it.

Your tax number also authorizes you to collect tax

Tax Numbers

when you sell merchandise. You must keep a record of all of the tax monies you take in and turn them over to the state. When the tax money is due varies from state to state and may also be dependent on how much business you're doing. For example, in some states if your sales are minimal, you're required to turn over the tax money you collect only once a year, but if your sales are brisk, the state will insist that you pay them on a quarterly basis. Of course, you won't be collecting tax from other dealers, but when you make a sale to a dealer, be sure to ask for and write down that dealer's state sales tax number.

If you're planning to go on any out-of-state buying trips, find out first if the state or states in which you're going to be antiques-hunting accepts sales tax numbers from your state. It may be worthwhile for you to apply for a sales tax number in the state you're planning to visit. Many dealers have tax numbers in several states.

We've met dealers who don't collect sales tax. Some of them have numbers but use them only to buy, making a token, usually quarterly, payment to the state so that their tax numbers won't be revoked. These dealers don't want to take the trouble to figure the sales tax and add it to the cost of the item being sold. Moreover, they feel that their customers resent having to pay sales tax on secondhand items. We've also met a few dealers who collect the tax but turn only a small portion of it over to the state. Both of these are illegal practices that we discourage strongly. In many states, tax agents roam the flea markets and antiques malls looking for dealers who fail to charge tax or to take dealers' tax numbers. Of course, collecting the tax and keeping it is an even more serious offense.

Federal Taxes

FEDERAL TAXES: RENDER UNTO CAESAR

While you are required to pay taxes to the state, this business gives you several legitimate breaks on your federal income tax. Although the rules change slightly from year to year, this is a business and you're entitled to take business deductions if you meet the requirements. You are allowed to deduct some expenses for the car or van you use to go to auction or flea markets, to haul goods to your market, and any other legitimate business use. However, you cannot deduct the miles you drive to and from the market so you can work there. You may deduct the rent you pay and the amount of money you have invested in inventory that tax year, balanced against your closing inventory and your sales. You may deduct rent paid for storage space for your antiques and collectibles.

There are dealers who carry large, impressive wads of bills in their pockets and pay cash for everything, accepting only cash for the merchandise purchased from them. They don't have tax numbers and don't acknowledge any profits. For all we know, they don't pay any income tax. All of this is illegal. The ramifications could, of course, be extremely serious. We keep our business strictly legal, and we urge you to do the same.

SET UP BOOKS: A PROFESSIONAL MUST

Keep an accurate record book. Accurate records are not only an asset at tax time, but enable you to tell on a week-to-week basis whether or not you're making money. While our record book covers everything we need to know, it's not complicated or involved. A three-ring notebook filled with

Set Up Books

lined paper with a divider does the job nicely. Take a ruler and make two approximately three quarter-inch columns on the left side. Now make a four-inch column, followed by four more three-quarter-inch columns. From left to right, head your columns as follows: *number* (we use the # sign), *dt in, description, pd., asked, got, dt sld.*

#	dt in	description	pd	asked	got	dt sold

Under the first column, put the number you assigned to the piece of merchandise you're entering. (More about numbering later in this chapter.) The second column is for the date you entered the merchandise into inventory. The third should describe the piece in as much detail as you can fit into the space allotted. The fourth is the amount you paid for the item. The fifth is the amount you're asking for it. Hopefully you'll be filling in the sixth within a short period of time with the amount for which you sold the article. And the last column is for the date on which it sold. We used to put the day, the month, and the year. But we've found for our purposes, it works just as well to list only the month and year.

The second section of the book should list your sales by the week. If you only keep the first part of the notebook, you'll find that after you've been in business for awhile you'll have to hunt through pages and pages to find when you sold any particular item, and tax time will be a nightmare.

Set up the second section of your notebook like this: divide a page into seven, three-quarter-inch columns. Label them *date, total sales, cost, profit, nontaxable, taxable,* and *tax* in that order. Each week, put the date in the left hand column and enter your week's sales in the columns across. This way you can tell at a glance what you sold each week, how much money you took in, how much tax you collected, and what your profits were.

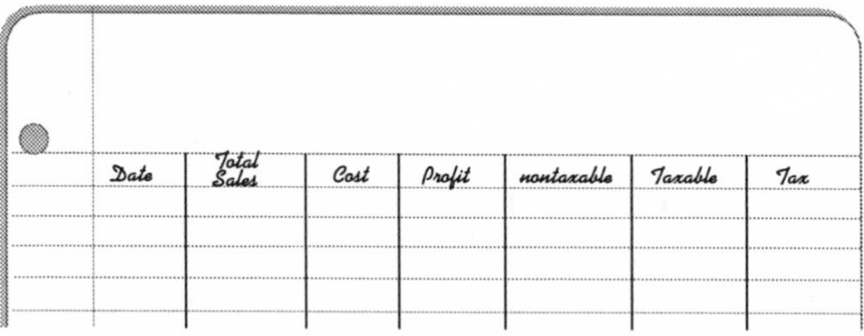

We also have a page at the very back of the notebook where we list expenses we incur for the business. These items, such as rent, tags, reference books, and so forth, are tax deductible. And they usually add up to a sizable deduction by the end of the year.

We take our book with us whenever we go to our co-op or any other place at which we sell or buy. It comes in handy if we purchase a piece and want to enter it immediately into inventory, placing it with our other merchandise. And then there are those times when we see an article for sale and remember that we once had one. But how much did we pay for it? How much did we sell it for? Did we have it long? Did we make a good profit on it? We have only to consult our book for the answers. Often we find that we didn't do well with a piece and so aren't interested in purchasing another one of the same type. But sometimes our book reveals that the article we've seen for sale is one that made us a handsome profit—something we're always happy to repeat.

PRICE IT AND MARK IT—ALL OF IT

You've bought it, you've lugged it home, you've cleaned it, you've admired it—but what price should you put on it? Pricing is an ongoing puzzle in this business; there are no hard and fast rules. If you have a specialty about which you are really knowledgeable, you'll have no trouble setting a price for merchandise that falls within its realm. You'll probably know exactly which customer will be interested in the pieces you buy. But most dealers don't specialize, and those that do generally don't handle that specialty exclusively. So it's back to the drawing board with pricing. There are wonderful (and not so wonderful) price guides to help you determine the worth of a myriad of items. The trouble is that there's an unwritten rule that says that no matter what you have bought, it won't be listed in the price guide you have at your fingertips. However, you can often find listings for things that are similar and use that as your guide.

The price you paid for an item will be a major factor in dictating what you'll be comfortable asking for it. No one anticipates taking a loss (although all dealers are forced to do so from time to time). Suppose you paid $20 for a

Roseville vase, and you're fortunate enough to find that exact vase listed. You see that it's valued in the book at $80. Great! You made a good buy. So are you going to ask $80 for the vase? Unless you want to sit with it for a long time, you're not. But you do want to at least double your money. (This is seldom possible with high-priced items, but it can usually be done with the less pricey merchandise.) So do you want to mark it at $40? That's double. But is it? Suppose you sell it to a dealer. Most dealers expect at least a ten percent courtesy discount. That means you're going to sell it for $36. And remember your rent comes out of your profits. So $50 seems to us like a good price to put on an item for which you paid $20 and that lists for $80. It's comfortable. A dealer can buy it from you and still make a profit. A retail customer can buy from you and still get a bargain. And, most important, you can make a profit.

We all end up with some merchandise about which we know virtually nothing. Sometimes it's an unusual piece that just looks interesting and different. Sometimes it's not what we thought it was when we purchased it. Pricing these items is a guessing game. This is one time we usually try to guess on the high side. What we have may be worth a great deal of money—or not. If we mark it at a low price because of our ignorance (and we have done this) it will probably be snapped up quickly by a more astute dealer. But if we mark it up and no one shows any interest in it, we can always adjust the price downward in small increments until we find a customer for it.

Collectibles are sometimes difficult to price. But if you determine the price at which some of the more modern

Price It; Mark It

collectibles, such as plates, were issued, it's helpful in establishing a value for your secondary market. We've found that the issuing companies, such as the Danbury Mint or the Franklin Mint, are most helpful in supplying original prices. Some of them will even tell you what a particular item is bringing on the secondary market. The Collector's Information Bureau in Grand Rapids, Michigan answers questions on the value of over 30,000 collectibles. They will provide pricing on bells, commemorative plates, prints, dolls, figurines, Christmas ornaments, and many other popular items produced by about 350 different companies. Their telephone number is 616-942-9CIB.

We purchase both string tags and tags with gummy backs. Whenever possible, we use the string tags but, of course, some things such as plates have no place to attach them. We've found that gummy tags often come unstuck after a length of time. And while we hope to sell our merchandise as soon as we put it out, this doesn't always happen. When string tags become worn looking, they're easy to replace. Gum tags leave a sticky residue that necessitates washing the article before applying a fresh tag. Some gummy tags stick better than others. We suggest purchasing a small number of tags until you find the ones that stay on the best.

We always mark our string tags on both sides. When merchandise is in a case, a tag often gets turned over so that the information on it can't be seen. A customer who's interested in a piece may be too shy to ask that a case be opened. He or she may figure that if the price isn't clearly visible, it's probably too high. It's our opinion that prices and other pertinent information should be easy to see.

What should you put on the tags? For one thing, this is where your numbering comes in. Assign a number to each item you buy. We advise starting at number 101. If you use number 1, it looks like you've just started in the business, and that might scare away customers. If your merchandise is at a co-op where you don't sell it yourself (at least not all the time), you're going to need some kind of code that will identify your articles from those belonging to the other dealers. In one of the markets where we now sell, the dealers use three letters for identification. Our tags are marked *DJB*. In addition, just to ensure that all sales are credited to the correct dealer, the tags have the booth number—in our case *12B*. So the upper left-hand corner of our tags read *DJB-12B*. We think this type of coding is a good idea even if you sell in a market where you staff your own booth all the time. Customers have been known to pick up an article in one booth and deposit it accidentally in another without either dealer seeing them do it. This personalized coding can prevent misunderstandings among dealers as to what belongs to whom.

The upper right-hand corner is where you put your merchandise identification number—the one you will have that piece of merchandise listed under in your record book. Underneath that number, in the body of the tag, write a brief description of the item. This is done for two reasons. First, you may be providing information about the piece that isn't obvious to someone looking at it. For instance, your tag might read, "sterling silver hairbrush." Wouldn't the brush be marked "sterling" if it were sterling? Yes, probably it would. But not necessarily in a conspicuous place. You might mark "Noritake" on the tag you put on a plate even though the backstamp clearly reads "Noritake." Your customers won't have to pick up the plate and turn it over to establish its identity.

There's another reason for identifying an object on the tag. Unfortunately, all customers aren't honest. Suppose you have two silver hairbrushes in your booth in a co-op. One is sterling silver, the other is silver plate. You have a price of $12 on the silver plated one and $25 on the sterling brush. In the area for description your tags each say only "Hairbrush." It's simple for a customer to slip the tags off and switch them, taking the sterling brush, which is now marked $12, to the cashier or salesperson. At the bottom of the tags, put the price you're asking for the item. If you're doing the selling yourself, you may want to add a code—usually into the number which you've given the item—that will tell you at a glance what the article cost you. For instance, your number on that sterling hair brush could read *101-21.* The 101 is your inventory number, and the 21 is the amount you paid for the brush—only backward. You could put *101-12,* but then an astute customer might figure that out. No one is going to think you paid $21 for a brush that you're hoping to sell for $25.

CREDIT CARDS: GOOD IDEA OR BAD?

Some dealers are set up to accept credit cards. This seemed like a good idea to us, so we applied for and got a Visa machine. We did this through our local bank, and they set up an account for us into which all Visa sales would be credited. Sounds good so far. We set up our machine and posted a card saying we accepted Visa. We only kept the account for three months. During those three months we did three transactions. Two of those transactions were for other dealers who didn't have Visa. The other one was for an amount over what could be charged without verification so we had to call to get permission to accept the charge. There was one phone—a pay phone—in the entire complex in which we were selling at the time. Don had gone to lunch so Joan had to ask another dealer to watch the booth while she went to make the phone call. There was a line waiting to use the phone. It took ten minutes to get to the head of the line, another three minutes or so to complete the call. The customer was not pleased to have been kept waiting, and we may have missed other sales by being absent from the booth. We agreed that the credit card service wasn't working out for us.

However, if you're dealing in very expensive merchandise, you probably should be set up to accept credit cards. Few retail buyers travel with large amounts of cash. There will, of course, be a fee that you will have to pay the credit card company for their services. You may decide it's a worthwhile expense or you may opt to pass the fee on to the customer as many dealers do.

CHECKS: TO ACCEPT OR NOT TO ACCEPT?

Someone is going out the door with that beautiful, ten-piece Limoges game set you prized so highly and all you have in return is a piece of paper—a check made out to you for $600. The check is drawn on a New York bank and you're in Pennsylvania—should you worry? Some dealers refuse to take out-of-state checks. Some dealers refuse to take any checks. We feel that despite the risks, you lose out on sales by not accepting checks. In the long run, you may forfeit a good deal of money. We accept checks from any state in the United States. Of course, if that sixth sense tells you, "This is a bad deal, I feel uneasy about this person," you can always say that you don't accept checks.

Checks

When you take a check from anyone, even if you know the person and have seen him or her around a great deal, get at least one form of identification. Ask to see a driver's license. Write the number and the state on the upper part of the face of the check or somewhere on the back of the check. Don't permit the customer to write the number for you and thus avoid showing you the license. Be sure that the check has the name and address of the person printed on it and look to see that it agrees with the name and address on the license. In all of the years we've been in business, we've never had a check bounce on us. But we certainly know other dealers who have lost out by taking a bad check.

In one instance, we sold a lovely Victorian rocking chair to a couple who said they were from New York. The chair was marked $500, and they didn't even ask for a better price. But they did say they'd have to pay by check. Their check didn't have an address on it, which they explained was because they were in the process of moving. For some reason, Joan, who was taking care of the financial end of the transaction, forgot to ask to see any identification. We were sure that we'd been had and the check would bounce. The fact that they hadn't asked for a discount heightened our suspicions—everyone in this business wants a price break. But we concluded this couple didn't ask for one because they didn't intend to pay for the chair. We were really paranoid about this one—and the check was fine. We were very lucky, and we never tested that luck again!

DEALER DISCOUNT: PROFESSIONAL COURTESY

It's standard practice throughout this business to offer a dealer discount. Generally the discount is ten percent. We often give a dealer a larger, sometimes much larger, discount. The size of the discount depends on several things. How long have we had the item? If we've been sitting with something for a year or more, we're anxious to get rid of it. Not only is it taking up space that could be filled with something else that, hopefully, would be more desirable to the customers in our market, but it's tying up money that we could use for other merchandise. There have been cases where we've sold an item to a dealer for what we paid for it—and were glad to do so.

Isn't it sort of a dirty trick to unload merchandise that hasn't moved on another, unsuspecting dealer? Not at all. He or she may take that merchandise to another market and sell it the next week for a handsome profit. Different items sell in different markets. We also discount merchandise to retail customers. But we don't always give them as big a break as we do dealers.

INVENTORY CONTROL AND RESTOCKING

Inventory Control and Restocking

Constantly keeping your merchandise new and interesting is essential to success in this business. But you can go broke buying if you're not selling. You need a formula for how much money to spend. But first open a checking account just for the business. If you mix antiques money in with your household money, you have to go through your books to know whether you're making a profit or not. And we found that before we kept our account separate, we tended to overspend on inventory.

There are several ways to approach your spending budget. We pay ourselves a salary out of our antiques account. We also pay the rent for our space, cover the cost of our supplies, and purchase our inventory from this account. Say we have $3,000 in the account on the first day of June. Our rent is $300 a month, so that leaves $2,700. If we pay ourselves $800, we have $1,900 left. We'd feel very comfortable spending $1,200 of that at the next auction we attended.

Another method is to put half of everything you take in back into merchandise. Subtract your rent from what's left and count the rest as profit. Many people favor this approach. Other dealers increase their inventories by recycling their initial investments. For example, if a dealer who uses this formula pays $30 for a table and sells it for $100, he'll count the $70 as pocket money and reinvest only the $30. We don't like this method because we like to keep upgrading our inventory. And if you're only willing to spend the amount of your original investment on inventory, it's difficult to increase the quality of your merchandise and still have enough of it to fill your space.

Presentation

PRESENTATION: BUSINESS CARDS AND STATIONERY

Business cards are inexpensive and establish you as a real business person. We suggest that every dealer get them. Cards can be made up with any design you want. You can have one drawn by an artist to your specifications, or you can select one from a large number of standard designs that the printers have to offer. Our card is white with a blue tree in the background and blue lettering over it. We think it's quite effective. You can select one with the colors featured in your booth. If you have blue tablecloths, perhaps you'd like blue and white business cards. If your merchandise is masculine, perhaps you'd do better with a bold, black print. A dealer with feminine, delicate merchandise might select scroll-type lettering.

We never put the address of our markets on our business cards. This is a transient business. We sell in several different places and never know how long we're going to stay in any one market. When a place doesn't work for us anymore, we look for another outlet. That's the beauty of not getting tied into a long lease. In addition, a customer can't always reach you at your market. It may be open only one day a week. And the management may frown on being asked to handle mail for individual dealers. In fact, you may never see a piece of mail addressed to you. Somehow, mail mysteriously disappears.

Printing the phone number of your outlet isn't a good idea either. If a customer wants to call you, he or she will have to do it during business hours. If your market is a co-op, you're probably not going to be there all the time that the outlet is open. We put our home phone number on our business cards. If you're not at home during the day, you might want to add something like, "Please call after 6:00 P.M." We never put our address on our cards because we pass them out to anyone who wants one. In fact, we leave a stack in each of our booths so customers may reach us directly about any item that interests them. This way, they do not have to try to work through the management, and we don't have strangers appearing on our doorstep.

Business stationery is expensive and, in most cases, not necessary. If you plan to do a large mail-order business, however, you might want to invest in some. Of course, you'll use your address and phone number. Many of today's sophisticated computers have a selection of fonts in various sizes with which you can design your own letterhead, printing envelopes to match.

With a little knowledge, a small investment, and a bit of determination, the antiques and collectibles business will work for anyone. We find it very rewarding to watch our profits grow while we have fun and learn more and more about antiques and collectibles.

APPENDIX I

United States Patent Numbers and Dates (through 1980)

Many collectibles, both old and newer, are marked with a patent number indicating the year in which the object was patented. This can be helpful in determining the age of the piece in question. Keep in mind, however, that it isn't necessarily the year in which the article you are investigating was made. Patent numbers are most helpful in proving that an item was manufactured after the year of the patent. For instance, if you see *Pat. No. 2,492,988*, it indicats that what you're looking at was made in 1950 or after that. The following are the patent numbers from 1836, when the patent office came into being, to 1980.

Year	Patent Numbers	Year	Patent Numbers
1836	1–10	1843	2,901–3,394
1837	110–545	1844	3,395–3,872
1838	546–1,105	1845	3,873–4,347
1839	1,106–1,464	1846	4,348–4,913
1840	1,465–1,922	1847	4,914–5,408
1841	1,923–2,412	1848	5,409–5,992
1842	2,413–2,900	1849	5,993–6,980

1850–
1907

Year	Patent Numbers	Year	Patent Numbers
1850	6,981–7,864	1879	211,078–223,210
1851	7,865–8,621	1880	223,211–236,136
1852	8,622–9,511	1881	236,137–251,684
1853	9,512–10,357	1882	251,685–269,819
1854	10,358–12,116	1883	269,820–291,015
1855	12,117–14,008	1884	291,016–310,162
1856	14,009–16,323	1885	310,163–333,493
1857	16,324–19,009	1886	333,494–355,290
1858	19,010–22,476	1887	355,291–375,719
1859	22,477–26,641	1888	375,720–395,304
1860	26,642–31,004	1889	395,305–418,664
1861	31,005–34,044	1890	418,665–443,986
1862	34,045–37,265	1891	443,987–466,314
1863	37,266–41,046	1892	466,315–488,975
1864	41,047–45,684	1893	488,976–511,743
1865	45,685–51,783	1894	511,744–531,618
1866	51,784–60,657	1895	531,619–552,501
1867	60,658–72,958	1896	552,502–574,368
1868	72,959–85,502	1897	574,369–596,466
1869	85,503–98,459	1898	596,467–616,870
1870	98,460–110,616	1899	616,871–640,166
1871	110,617–122,303	1900	640,167–664,826
1872	122,304–134,503	1901	664,827–690,384
1873	134,504–146,119	1902	690,385–717,520
1874	146,120–158,349	1903	717,521–748,566
1875	158,350–171,640	1904	748,567–778,833
1876	171,641–185,812	1905	778,834–808,617
1877	185,813–198,732	1906	808,618–839,798
1878	198,733–211,077	1907	839,799–875,678

1908–
1965

Year	Patent Numbers	Year	Patent Numbers
1908	875,679–908,435	1937	2,066,309–2,104,003
1909	908,436–945,009	1938	2,104,004–2,142,079
1910	945,010–980,177	1939	2,142,080–2,185,169
1911	980,178–1,013,094	1940	2,185,170–2,227,417
1912	1,013,095–1,049,325	1941	2,227,418–2,268,539
1913	1,049,326–1,083,266	1942	2,268,540–2,307,006
1914	1,083,267–1,123,211	1943	2,307,007–2,338,080
1915	1,123,212–1,166,418	1944	2.338,081–2,366,153
1916	1,166,419–1,210,388	1945	2,336,154–2,391,855
1917	1,210,389–1,251,457	1946	2,391,856–2,413,674
1918	1,251,458–1,290,026	1947	2,413,675–2,433,823
1919	1,290,027–1,326,898	1948	2,433,824–2,457,796
1920	1,326,899–1,364,062	1949	2,457,797–2,492,943
1921	1,364,063–1,401,947	1950	2,492,944–2,536,015
1922	1,401,948–1,440,361	1951	2,536,016–2,580,378
1923	1,440,362–1,478,995	1952	2,580,379–2,624,045
1924	1,478,996–1,521,589	1953	2,624,046–2,664,561
1925	1,521,590–1,568,039	1954	2,664,562–2,698,433
1926	1,568,040–1,612,699	1955	2,698,434–2,728,912
1927	1,612,700–1,654,520	1956	2,728,913–2,775,761
1928	1,654,521–1,696,896	1957	2,775,762–2,818,566
1929	1,696,897–1,742,180	1958	2,818,567–2,866,972
1930	1,742,181–1,787,423	1959	2,866,973–2,919,442
1931	1,787,424–1,839,189	1960	2,919,443–2,966,680
1932	1,839,190–1,892,662	1961	2,966,681–3,015,102
1933	1,892,663–1,941,448	1962	3,015,103–3,070,800
1934	1,941,449–1,985,877	1963	3,070,801–3,116,486
1935	1,985,878–2,026,515	1964	3,116,487–3,163,864
1936	2,026,516–2,066,308	1965	3,163,865–3,226,728

1966–1980

Year	Patent Numbers
1966	3,226,729–3,295,142
1967	3,295,143–3,360,799
1968	3,360,800–3,419,906
1969	3,419,907–3,487,469
1970	3,487,470–3,551,908
1971	3,551,909–3,631,538
1972	3,631,539–3,707,728
1973	3,707,729–3,781,913
1974	3,781,914–3,858,240
1975	3,858,241–3,930,270
1976	3,930,271–4,000,519
1977	4,000,520–4,065,811
1978	4,065,812–4,131,951
1979	4,131,952–4,180,866
1980	4,180,867–4,242,757

APPENDIX II

Price Guides and Other References

Price Guides

Three major price guides are published annually. We recommend that you purchase each of them every year:

Kovels' Antiques and Collectibles Price List, Crown.

Schroeder's Antiques Price Guide, Collector Books.

Warman's Antiques and Their Prices, Warman's Publishing.

Miller's International Antiques Price Guide, published by Viking Studio Books, is a beautiful annual publication with a photograph of each item that's listed. The merchandise portrayed is of the highest quality. We treat ourselves to a Miller's every couple of years, but we rarely come across any articles that are listed there.

The following is a list of a few of the specialized price guides that may be of interest to you. If they're not available through your bookstore, you can order them from the publishers.

Aladdin Electric Lamps. J. W. Courter. Des Moines, Iowa: Plain Talk, 1987.

All about Paperweights. Lawrence H. Selman. Rutland, Vermont: Charles E. Tuttle Co., Inc., 1992.

American Belleek. Mary Frank Gaston. Paducah, Kentucky: Collector Books, 1989.

Antique and Collectible Thimbles and Accessories. Averil Mathis. Paducah, Kentucky: Collector Books, 1989.

Antique Brass Identification and Values. Mary Frank Gaston. Paducah, Kentucky: Collector Books, 1985.

Antique Copper Identification and Values. Mary Frank Gaston. Paducah, Kentucky: Collector Books, 1985.

Antique Purses. Richard Holiner. Paducah, Kentucky: Collector Books, 1990.

Collectible German Animals Value Guide 1948–1968. Dee Hockenberry. Cumberland, Maryland: Hobby House, 1989.

Collector's Encyclopedia of Disneyana. Davic Longest and Michael Stern. Paducah, Kentucky: Collector Books, 1992.

Collector's Encyclopedia of Heisey Glass 1925–1938. Neila Bredehoft. Paducah, Kentucky: Collector Books, 1989.

Collector's Encyclopedia of Roseville Pottery. Sharon and Bob Huxford. Paducah, Kentucky: Collector Books, 1989.

Collector's Guide to Art Deco. Mary Frank Gaston. Paducah, Kentucky: Collector Books, 1989.

Collector's Guide to Cartoon and Promotional Drinking Glasses. John Hervey. Gas City, Indiana: L-W Books, 1992.

Collector's Guide to Country Baskets. Don and Carol Raycraft. Paducah, Kentucky: Collector Books, 1990.

Collector's Information Bureau Collectibles Price Guide. Diane Carnevale. Radnor, Pennsylvania: Wallace Homestead, 1992.

Comics Values Annual: The Comic Book Price Guide. Alex Malloy. Radnor, Pennsylvania: Wallace Homestead, 1992.

Cookie Jars. Ermagene Westfall. Paducah, Kentucky: Collector Books, 1991.

Electric Lighting of the 20s and 30s. James Edward Black, ed. Gas City, Indiana: L-W Books, 1988.

Games: American Games and Their Makers, 1882–1992, with Values. Brue Whitehill. Radnor, Pennsylvania: Wallace Homestead, 1992.

A Guide to Collecting Cookbooks. Colonel Bob Allen. Paducah, Kentucky: Collector Books, 1990.

Hakes' Guide to Presidential Campaign Collectibles. Ted Hake. Radnor, Pennsylvania: Wallace Homestead, 1992.

Hat Pins and Hat Pin Holders. Lillian Baker. Paducah, Kentucky: Collector Books, 1988.

Head Vases Identification and Values. Kathleen Cole. Paducah, Kentucky: Collector Books, 1989.

Jessop International Blue Book, 3rd ed. Douglas St. Denny. Radnor, Pennsylvania: Wallace Homestead, 1992.

Kovels' Illustrated Price Guide to Royal Doulton. Ralph and Terry Kovel. New York: Crown, 1984.

Majolica Pottery. Mariann K. Marks. Paducah, Kentucky: Collector Books, 1989.

Official Identification and Price Guide to Movie Memorabilia. Richard De Thuin. New York: House of Collectibles, 1989.

Official Identification and Price Guide to Vintage Clothing. Cynthia Giles. New York: House of Collectibles, 1989.

Official Price Guide to Collectible Toys. Richard Friz. New York: House of Collectibles, 1987.

Official Price Guide to Collector Plates. Gene Ehlert. New York: House of Collectibles, 1988.

Official Price Guide to Paperbacks and Magazines. Charles and Donna Jordan. New York: House of Collectibles, 1986.

Official Price Guide to Peanuts. Freddi Margolis and Andrea Podley. New York: House of Collectibles, 1990.

Oil Lamps: The Kerosene Era in North America, Updated Prices. Catherine M. V. Thuro. Radnor, Pennsylvania: Wallace Homestead, 1992.

Oriental Antiques and Art. Sandra Andacht. Radnor, Pennsylvania: Wallace Homestead, 1987.

A Price Guide to Wallace Nutting Pictures. Michael Ivankovich. Doylestown, Pennsylvania: Diamond Press, 1989.

Railroad Collectibles. Stanley L. Baker. Paducah, Kentucky: Collector Books, 1985.

R. Atkinson Fox—His Life and Work. Rita C. Mortenson. Radnor, Pennsylvania: Wallace Homestead, 1985.

Tomart's Price Guide to Garage Sale Gold. Bob Welbaum, ed. Radnor, Pennsylvania: Wallace Homestead, 1992.

Tuttle Dictionary of Antiques & Collectibles Terms. Don & Joan Bingham. Rutland, Vermont: Charles E. Tuttle Co., Inc., 1992.

The Value Guide to Antique Oak Furniture. Conover Hill. Paducah, Kentucky: Collector Books, 1987.

Wallace Homestead Price Guide to Plastic Collectibles, Updated Prices. Lynda Stewart McNulty. Radnor, Pennsylvania: Wallace Homestead, 1992.

Warman's Country Antiques and Collectibles. Dana N. Marykin and Harry L. Rinker, eds. Radnor, Pennsylvania: Wallace Homestead, 1992.

Warman's English and Continental Pottery and Porcelain. Susan D. Bagdade and Allen D. Bagdade. Willow Grove, Pennsylvania: Warman's, 1987.

Warman's Oriental Antiques. Gloria and Robert Mascarelli. Radnor, Pennsylvania: Warman's, 1992.

Wedgewood: A Guide for the Collector. Radnor, Pennsylvania: Wallace Homestead, 1992.

Wicker Furniture Styles and Prices. Robert W. and Harriet Swedberg. Radnor, Pennsylvania: Wallace Homestead, 1988.

The World of Barbie Dolls. Paris and Susan Manos. Paducah, Kentucky: Collector Books, 1990.